Across an Untamed Land:

The Lewis and Clark Expedition

A Story of Discovery, Survival, and

The Birth of the American West

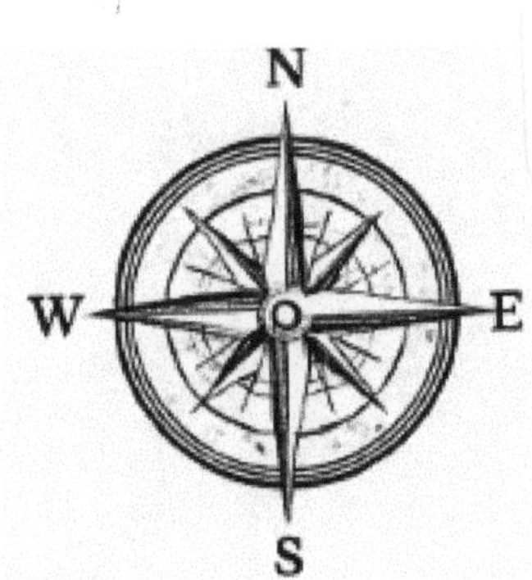

Blake Whitworth

© 2026 **Blake Whitworth**

All rights reserved. No part of this book may be reproduced, stored in a retrieval system, or transmitted in any form or by any means—electronic, mechanical, photocopying, recording, or otherwise—without prior written permission of the publisher, except for brief quotations used in reviews, academic works, or scholarly analysis.

This book is a work of nonfiction. Every effort has been made to ensure accuracy in the research, historical facts, and details presented. Some dialogue, scenes, and characterization have been selectively dramatized for narrative readability while maintaining historical integrity.

Printed in the United States of America

First Edition

Contents

Introduction

THE RIVER WAS swollen and cold, its gray surface roiling under the weight of spring rains. The men of the Corps of Discovery gripped their oars, muscles aching. Captain Meriwether Lewis called out from the lead pirogue as a log, half-submerged, hurtled downstream. Behind him, William Clark scanned the banks for signs of a safe landing. Sacagawea, holding her infant son, watched the sky for breaks in the clouds. York, Clark's enslaved man, steadied the boat, his eyes fixed  on the white water ahead. It was May 1805, and the expedition was fighting its way up the Missouri, deeper into a land most Americans had only guessed at. Each paddle stroke pushed them further from what they knew, and closer to something that would change the country forever.

This book tells the story of that journey. It is for curious readers of all ages. It is for families who want to explore together, for students and teachers in classrooms, and for anyone who loves American history. It is also for those who seek not just facts, but stories—stories of real people facing real dangers, making hard choices, and sometimes failing. There will be triumphs—the first glimpse of the Pacific, the successful crossing of the Rockies, the moments when teamwork carried the day. But you will also see the hardships: hunger, illness, biting cold, and the ever-present fear of the unknown. You will hear from Sacagawea and York, from the Native leaders who aided—and sometimes challenged—the Corps, and from the ordinary men whose names rarely appear in textbooks. Let us set out together, across an untamed land, and see what waits beyond the next bend in the river.

Chapter 1: Seeds of Discovery – Setting the Stage for an Epic Journey

In the spring of 1803, President Thomas Jefferson sent Meriwether Lewis a letter dense with instructions and hope—an invitation not just for a job but to cross the boundary of the known world. That same spring, Congress buzzed with rumors. Some said France had sold half a continent for less than three cents an acre; others talked of Spanish spies, wild lands with monsters and gold, and the fate of American farmers and fur traders. Newspapers in Philadelphia printed maps filled with blank spaces. In taverns up and down the coast, men debated where the Mississippi actually ended and what might lie beyond. The United States, once small and Atlantic-bound, was now stretching westward, uncertain but eager for more. The story of Lewis and Clark begins not with two captains on a riverbank, but in Jefferson's imagination—with a dream as boundless as the land itself.

Jefferson's Vision – The Louisiana Purchase and the Birth of the Expedition

Thomas Jefferson thrived on questions. As a boy, he collected fossils and sketched birds; as president, he filled his study with mammoth bones, globes, and books from across Europe. He believed knowledge could improve lives and saw America as an

"empire for liberty," though he constantly worried about threats: French troops in New Orleans, Spanish forts by the Rio Grande, British trappers moving south from Canada. His letters reveal equal parts wonder and anxiety over what might happen if foreign powers claimed the lands west of the Mississippi.

When news spread that Napoleon Bonaparte wanted to restore France's empire in North America, Jefferson responded swiftly. He sent James Monroe to Paris, hoping only to buy New Orleans and a bit of land for American commerce. Napoleon, however, offered the entire Louisiana

Territory—an expanse doubling the size of the United States for $15 million, or roughly 827,000 square miles (more land than France, Spain, Portugal, Italy, Germany, and Switzerland combined. Congress reacted with mixed emotions. Some cheered, others called it reckless. New Englanders feared their influence would wane, while Westerners saw new opportunities.

Even Jefferson admitted "doubts whether this is not beyond the constitutional powers vested in me," but he approved the purchase. Suddenly, a vast new map was filled with unknowns. No one was certain what mountains, rivers, peoples, or resources the land held. Jefferson's curiosity surged. He wanted scientific data—samples of plants, animals, even fossils, new to European science. He sought reports on Indigenous nations, their customs, languages, and trade networks, and wanted to establish peaceful relationships for future American trade.

There was ongoing talk of a "Northwest Passage"—a water route possibly connecting the Mississippi to the Pacific. Jefferson told Lewis, "The object of your mission is to explore the Missouri River & such principal stream of it as…may offer the most direct & practicable water communication across this continent for the purposes of commerce."

Maps from Europe were mostly wild guesses between St. Louis and Oregon, often filled with fanciful drawings of mammoths or volcanoes. For many Americans, these were mythic and promising lands—but understanding them required action, not just dreams.

Jefferson's vision was more than scientific or economic; it was national. He believed Americans were meant to spread across the continent, bringing new government and liberty with them—a belief later known as Manifest Destiny. Yet even then, people recognized its cost; discovery for some meant dispossession for others. In 1803, Jefferson wrote: "The acquisition of territory is to be considered as an extension of our principles." But beneath his boldness was caution: great changes brought risk of conflict as well as opportunity.

The Louisiana Purchase marked a turning point not just on maps, but in national identity, forcing Americans to consider what their country would become: adventurous or careful, inclusive or exclusive, guided by science or superstition. The need to explore these new lands was urgent—not just for wealth and glory, but for understanding what it meant to occupy this new landscape.

Assembling the Corps of Discovery – Recruiting a Diverse Team

Building the Corps of Discovery was not a task for the faint-hearted or the indecisive. Meriwether Lewis, with Jefferson's blessing, began searching for people who could withstand grueling days and unpredictable nights, endure discomfort, and still think clearly when the stakes rose. The criteria were strict: each recruit needed physical strength, proven endurance, and the ability to adapt to changing conditions without complaint. Lewis wanted skilled hunters who could track game in deep woods, blacksmiths who could forge and repair tools on the fly, and men who understood the land and water. Technical knowledge mattered, but so did grit and a willingness to cooperate with strangers.

Lewis looked for men who could work as a team—fiercely loyal when it counted, but independent enough to make tough calls in the wild. Diversity wasn't just an afterthought; it was a practical necessity. The Corps included men from military backgrounds, but also French-Canadian voyageurs—boatmen used to the treacherous rivers of North America. Their expertise in managing canoes through swift currents was unmatched. These voyageurs spoke French, blended European and Native influences, and knew how to barter, laugh, and survive far from home. Interpreters joined as well, bridging languages and cultures, making it possible for the Corps to meet tribes along the Missouri and beyond with some chance of understanding.

Skilled hunters were prized—none more so than George Drouillard, a man of Shawnee and French descent, whose abilities with a rifle and knowledge of sign language made him indispensable. York's place in the expedition stands out in American history. Enslaved since birth, York belonged to William Clark but was trusted as a full participant on this mission. He towered over many of his peers—strong, resourceful, and often tasked with the hardest labor.

Records show Native nations were surprised to see a Black man as part of the Corps; some even believed he possessed special powers. Despite being denied freedom or pay, York's presence shaped many encounters, from portages to councils with tribal chiefs. Trust grew slowly among these men. Some had never met before gathering at Camp Dubois during the winter of 1803–1804.

The group included John Ordway, a sergeant known for steady leadership and patient record-keeping. Ordway was often the one who kept morale up when tempers flared or supplies ran low. Patrick Gass, a carpenter with an eye for detail, would later become vital in building forts and repairing boats—his quick thinking often meant the difference between comfort and misery. Drouillard's sharp instincts made him the best scout; he could disappear into the woods for days, then return with fresh meat or news of nearby tribes. Military discipline formed the backbone of daily life, but it wasn't enough by itself.

The Corps needed frontier know-how—practical wisdom gathered from years spent trapping, trading, farming, or fighting along the expanding edge of America. Orders from Lewis or Clark mattered, but so did the judgment of men like Gass and Drouillard when faced with flooded rivers or unknown animal tracks. This blend of structure and improvisation helped the Corps confront hardship without falling apart. Tensions sometimes simmered beneath the surface. Not everyone trusted each other at first. Soldiers chafed under orders; voyageurs sometimes resented strict rules; interpreters bridged not just language but also attitude and custom. Yet moments of crisis—whether a sudden bear charge or a near-mutiny—forced everyone to depend on one another. A single mistake could mean disaster; a shared effort brought hope.

The official records from this time reveal flashes of personality and pride. Gass described the early days as "cold and disagreeable," but praised his comrades' resolve. Ordway noted in his journal that "all hands appeared willing to encounter every difficulty." Drouillard's scouting made him legendary even among tough men; Clark wrote he was "always ready, always willing." York's story rarely appeared in official documents except as Clark's "servant," yet oral histories from Native groups recall his presence vividly.

The team's mix of backgrounds foreshadowed both challenges and strengths. Each man brought different skills: crafting dugouts on the Missouri's banks, trading with tribes for food or horses, patching wounds after accidents or fights. They needed each other in ways city folk seldom understand—a lesson still true for anyone who has ever relied on strangers in hard times.

Meriwether Lewis stood out in any crowd, but not because of loud words or bold gestures. He grew up in Virginia, restless and curious, with a mind always turning toward questions about the world. As a young man, he joined the Army, but his real education came at Monticello under the eye of Thomas Jefferson. Jefferson saw in Lewis a kindred spirit—a lover of plants, animals, and the kind of scientific puzzles that could keep a person up at night. Lewis liked to wander the woods alone, studying birds or sketching wildflowers.

He read books on geology, medicine, and navigation. His handwriting in journals strikes you as careful, sometimes almost hesitant, as if he weighed each word. He battled periods of melancholy, yet his drive for accuracy and understanding set him apart. People often describe Lewis as intense, deeply introspective, and driven by inner storms that rarely showed on his face.

William Clark brought a different energy to the table. Born into a large frontier family in Kentucky, Clark was used to hard work and harder living. He had command experience on the western borderlands, leading men through both Indian country and wild forests. He could build a fort, break a wild horse, or lead a hunt for days without losing his cool. Clark's writing feels brisker, more direct—lists of supplies, sketches of camp layouts, notes on daily progress. He always seemed to know what needed doing next. Soldiers respected him because he listened as much as he talked. His style was practical and hands-on; he solved problems by rolling up his sleeves. If Lewis pondered possibilities, Clark found solutions.

Their leadership styles could not have been more different, yet that difference proved their greatest strength. Lewis would pore over details in the evening: lists of specimens collected, calculations of latitude by starlight, plans for the next day's diplomacy or data collection. He sometimes worried over mistakes or decisions long after others had gone to sleep. Clark woke up early, checked on the men and equipment, and made sure breakfast fires were burning. When storms hit, or tempers flared, Clark stepped forward—steady and unflappable—while Lewis focused on the bigger picture. Lewis's scientific training made him cautious; Clark's frontier savvy made him quick on his feet. Where one hesitated, the other pressed on.

They balanced each other in ways few partnerships do. When facing unknown rapids or tense negotiations with tribal chiefs, their different approaches blended: Lewis would seek out information and try to predict outcomes; Clark would manage the immediate risks and keep morale high. Sometimes Lewis's self-doubt threatened to paralyze him—Clark would step in with encouragement or a joke to break the tension. In turn, Clark sometimes moved too quickly; Lewis reined him back just enough to avoid reckless choices. Side by side, their friendship grew deeper with every hardship faced together. The decision to grant Clark "equal command" was more than a courtesy; it was a statement about what this expedition needed to succeed. Technically, only Lewis reported directly to President Jefferson, but from the start, he asked that Clark be recognized as a co-leader in every way that mattered. This move was unusual for the time—Army hierarchy ran strictly, but Lewis trusted Clark completely and saw that the scale of their mission required two heads, not one. Giving Clark equal rank was also a social gamble; some officers grumbled about blurred lines of authority. The men responded with respect—they saw two captains who led not by force or title alone but by example and shared hardship.

Behind closed doors and on paper, you see evidence of their bond in early letters they exchanged while planning the expedition. They wrote about supplies, maps, and men—not just as officers but as friends who understood each other's strengths and fears. Both sacrificed personal comfort: Lewis left behind the relative safety of Washington's political circles; Clark gave up the chance to settle down with family or pursue a more predictable military career. Each faced uncertainty about the dangers ahead, but stayed committed because they trusted each other more than anyone else.

Lewis's loyalty to Jefferson burned bright but was matched by his loyalty to Clark; Clark's sense of duty ran both to his friend and to the men under his care. Together, they created an atmosphere where every member of the Corps felt their leaders would not ask more than they would give themselves. Their partnership became a model—two minds working as one, blending introspection with action, caution with boldness. That rare chemistry kept their mission moving forward even when hope ran thin. Their friendship wasn't just professional; it ran deeper than shared orders or mutual respect. It was built on countless small moments—shared meals after long days, whispered fears traded at midnight campfires, jokes that eased tension after near disaster.

Preparing for the Unknown – Supplies, Trade Goods, and Scientific Tools

Packing for the expedition was nothing like preparing for a weekend hike or even the longest camping trip you can imagine. Picture trying to predict every need, every threat, every possible encounter, for a group of over thirty men—plus a dog and, soon enough, a baby—headed into a landscape with no stores, no backup, and not even a reliable map. Lewis faced days and nights making lists, crossing out items, adding new ones as doubts crept in. He worried about food: how much would be enough? They would need barrels of salted pork and flour, kegs of whiskey, dried beans, parched corn, and portable soup (a kind of condensed broth that could last for years).

Weapons took up as much space as provisions: rifles, powder horns, lead balls, tomahawks, knives, and spare flints. Medical supplies were precious—lancets for bloodletting, jars of mercury (then believed to cure many ills), herbal remedies, even tooth powder and combs. Each item had to earn its place. Too little meant starvation or defeat; too much could sink a boat in the shallows.

The official packing list Lewis crafted reads like a mix between a survival manual and a general store inventory. It included tents made of oiled linen to keep rain at bay, mosquito curtains for the feverish Midwest summers, and heavy wool blankets to fight off the northern chill. He packed sewing needles, awls, thread, and shoes that could be mended on the move.

They brought axes and saws for building shelters or boats, and even a small corn mill to grind whatever grain they could find or trade. With every line on his list, Lewis faced his own anxieties—what if they needed something no one had thought to bring? What if winter came early or game ran scarce? He tried to imagine every scenario. Trade goods were not an afterthought but the linchpin of diplomacy.

The Corps would meet dozens of Native nations along the way; each encounter could mean safe passage or sudden danger. To prepare, they packed an array of items designed to impress and build trust: peace medals stamped with Jefferson's image, strings of glass beads in bright colors, small mirrors that caught sunlight and curiosity alike, bolts of calico cloth, brass kettles that gleamed in the firelight, vermilion pigment for painting faces or gifts, and tomahawks that doubled as both weapons and ceremonial tokens.

These were more than gifts—they were tools for signaling respect, forging alliances, and smoothing over misunderstandings. Lewis knew that one well-timed present could open doors or save lives. The medals in particular symbolized a new relationship with the United States—a promise written in metal rather than words.

Scientific goals shaped nearly every choice. Jefferson wanted more than stories; he wanted data—facts that would stand up to scrutiny back in Philadelphia or Paris. Lewis packed sextants for measuring angles between stars and the horizon; chronometers to track longitude with precision;

compasses sensitive enough to find direction on cloudy nights; thermometers for logging temperature swings from river valley to mountain pass; and specimen jars for insects, seeds, or river water that might reveal hidden life. Glass vials held soil samples; plant presses flattened wildflowers between sheets of paper for later study.

Each instrument was delicate yet vital—a broken lens or jammed lock could mean lost knowledge. Lewis also included writing desks that folded into trunks so he could jot down observations by candlelight. These journals became a kind of backbone for the entire expedition: a living record of what they saw, felt, ate, and feared. The keelboat itself reflected hours of innovation and worry. Built in Pittsburgh to Lewis's exacting specifications, it boasted a reinforced hull for the Missouri's snags and sandbars, hidden compartments for storing trade goods out of sight, a collapsible mast for sailing with favorable winds, and even a tiny deck cannon as a last resort.

The boat carried desks for writing reports and maps on water-stained parchment; each officer had his own case for pencils, ink powder, and sealing wax. Improvisation was constant: when something broke or ran out—rope frayed by sharp rocks, boots worn through after days of portage—the men stopped to patch or invent solutions on the fly.

Every decision about supplies revealed both priorities and fears. Lewis's careful packing betrayed his nervousness about what lay ahead, but also his deep respect for knowledge—he wanted to come back with answers no one else had. The trade goods showed he understood people would matter as much as rivers or mountains. The tools for observation proved that science was not some luxury but a lifeline: proof they had been there and learned something lasting.

Mapping the Great Unknown – Early Cartography and Route Planning

Maps in 1803 looked more like dreams than facts. If you opened an atlas, you'd see the Mississippi River flowing like a thick black ribbon, then everything west of St. Louis faded into guesses. Blank spaces stretched for hundreds of miles. Some maps showed chains of mountains where there were only rolling plains; others drew fantastical rivers joining the Atlantic to the Pacific, as if the continent were a simple puzzle waiting to be solved. European cartographers filled their pages with dotted lines, question marks, and invented lakes.

In Paris and London, men who had never crossed the Atlantic drew wild curves and labeled them "Great River of the West" or "Mountains of Bright Stones." They relied on secondhand tales from trappers, Native traders, or shipwrecked sailors, blending myth and hearsay with wishful thinking. One year, a Spanish map might claim a single river cut across the Rockies; the next, British maps would erase it. America's own surveyors tried to correct errors, but without real exploration, their efforts only added to the confusion.

The uncertainty in these maps did more than frustrate scholars. It shaped national policy and everyday decisions. If you were a farmer thinking about moving west, you faced a wall of rumors—stories of monstrous animals, impassable deserts, or golden cities hidden in forests.

For politicians like Jefferson, these blank spaces were both thrilling and dangerous: they offered hope for expansion but also risked war or disaster if Americans wandered blindly into Spanish or British claims. The need for accurate maps became urgent. Jefferson's scientific approach set a new standard. He instructed Lewis to measure latitude and longitude at every major stop, making sure future explorers could trace their steps and avoid disaster. Jefferson's orders were detailed: record river widths, note the soil's quality, observe plant life, animals, minerals, and report weather patterns.

Natural features mattered not just for science but for farmers and traders eager to follow. He told Lewis to describe "the face of the country," noting everything from hill shapes to the color of the earth. These instructions reflected Enlightenment thinking—truth should be observed, measured, recorded, not guessed at or imagined.

To prepare for this monumental task, Lewis underwent an intense crash course in Philadelphia. He studied with leading mathematicians and astronomers—men like Andrew Ellicott and Robert Patterson—learning how to use sextants and octants to find positions by reading the stars. Lewis practiced calculating longitude using chronometers, a tricky art since any small error could send future travelers miles off course. He studied minerals with chemists and learned how to press plants for botanical samples.

In workshops and lecture halls, he asked endless questions about surveying equipment—how to keep compasses accurate in wild weather, when to trust a barometer or thermometer, which ink would best survive rain and rough handling.

These skills became second nature as he ran practice expeditions down the Ohio River, logging distances between bends, timing currents, and testing his notes against known points. Mapping wasn't just about lines on paper—it was an act of imagination backed by hard science. Jefferson dreamed of finding a "Northwest Passage," a water route connecting the interior of North America to the Pacific Ocean. The idea had haunted explorers since Columbus—if such a passage existed, it would transform trade and power forever. Many believed rivers must link up behind the Rockies; others clung to stories from Native guides or fur traders who claimed they had seen distant waters flowing west. Lewis carried these hopes with him but also planned for disappointment.

 Each day on the river meant taking measurements, sketching new bends, debunking old myths. This mixture of myth and observation shaped every decision about route planning. The Corps studied old French fur trade journals for hints about where rivers split, or mountains rose. They weighed stories of "portages" where canoes could be dragged from one watershed to another—a crucial shortcut if it existed. Practical questions pressed in: How wide was each valley? Where did buffalo roam? Which places looked promising for future settlements or forts?

During this period, mapping took on an almost sacred quality—a record not just of place but of ambition and hope. Each time Lewis raised his sextant at dusk, or Clark traced a new river curve by lantern light, they chipped away at centuries of error and speculation. Their maps would prove more valuable than gold for those who followed: pioneers, merchants, ranchers, and even scientists eager to study America's wildest places.

In many ways, mapping the continent was like exploring a story half-written in invisible ink. Each observation revealed new facts while erasing old fictions. The Corps approached each day with pencils sharpened but eyes wide open for surprises—the kind that could shift not just maps but destinies.

Native Nations of the West – Understanding the Lands to be Crossed

Before Lewis and Clark set out, they faced a land rich with established Native nations, not uninhabited wilderness. The Mandan and Hidatsa built bustling earth-lodge villages along the upper Missouri, thriving through agriculture, trade, and strong communities. These towns were lively, with corn drying, children at play, and elders sharing stories. North and east, the Sioux (Dakota, Lakota, Nakota) controlled vast grasslands, growing in power with each season as their horse culture matured and alliances shifted.

Farther west, the Shoshone ranged mountain valleys, expert horsepeople braving harsh terrain. Along the Snake and Columbia Rivers, the Nez Perce and Chinook fished and traded, their societies molded by salmon runs and cedar forests. Many more—Arikara, Blackfeet, Flathead, Umatilla—each held distinct languages, traditions, and histories.

Jefferson's guidance mixed respect with ambition: "Treat them in the most friendly and conciliatory manner which their own conduct will admit." The Corps of Discovery would act as both guests and agents of change, acutely aware that behind each interaction, American expansion loomed. Peace medals—silver tokens with Jefferson's likeness—became symbols of alliance. Beads, ribbons, and flags were distributed in ceremonies aimed to impress or build goodwill, yet gifts could not resolve deeper questions regarding land, hunting grounds, or trust. Each exchange risked misunderstanding.

Indigenous societies were layered and diverse. The Mandan farmed fertile river bottoms, maintaining detailed oral histories. The Hidatsa formed alliances through marriage and trade. The Sioux held influence through numbers and military strength, though their bands often debated matters of peace and war. The Shoshone endured scarcity, excelling in mobility. Nez Perce decisions required consensus, while Chinook traders prospered through dealings with coastal visitors.

These groups spoke distinct languages, sometimes related, often very different, following seasonal patterns rooted in tradition. Rivalries and old grievances sometimes resurfaced in conflicts over land or stolen horses. Communication was vital. Interpreters—Native, French, and those of mixed ancestry— became indispensable, translating not just words but customs and intentions. Sometimes four or more languages were needed to connect a Corps leader and a tribal elder. Cultural brokers like Sacagawea quietly bridged worlds, with her presence often proving crucial in councils. Lewis and Clark relied on these go-betweens to interpret subtle cues: a pause before accepting a pipe, where gifts were placed, and who entered the lodge first.

Long before Americans arrived, Native societies were already changing in response to distant wars and new technologies. Horses, brought north from Spanish settlements, revolutionized hunting, travel, and warfare. Guns reached them from French and British traders, altering power balances. Disease, especially smallpox, devastated villages, leaving lasting gaps in leadership and family structures. Some elders remembered a time before horses or steel; younger warriors embraced these changes, yet struggled with their impact.

Trade networks wove these nations together before Lewis and Clark's journey. Mandan villages served as trade hubs for goods from Mexico to Hudson Bay—shells, copper, cloth, tobacco. British and French traders competed for furs and alliances, while Spanish agents attempted to draw tribes south. By 1804, Americans were new players in an established system. Their arrival promised new goods—and new threats to long-held lands.

U.S. ambitions could not help but disrupt this complex world. To Jefferson, commerce was a bridge to peace and evidence of U.S. expansion westward. Every gift hid an agenda: opening trade routes, gathering intelligence, and encouraging Native peoples to regard the U.S. as a friend. But trust was fragile; misunderstandings or unkept promises could provoke violence beyond what peace medals could remedy. Alliances among nations shifted constantly—like rivers—trust was earned through deeds, not words. The Corps of Discovery would find that survival depended as much on listening as leading, on recognizing Native nations not as obstacles but as sovereign powers shaping their own destiny.

Crossing these lands demanded humility, patience, and a willingness to learn from those who knew them best. The Corps' journey would rely on all three, revealing how much Americans had yet to understand about the world beyond their borders.

Chapter 2: Into the Current – The Missouri River and the First Encounters

Aboard the Keelboat – Life on the Water Begins

Imagine the sun not yet risen, but already the air is thick with the sound of boots thumping on damp earth and whispered orders in the gray light. Each morning began before dawn for you and every member of the Corps. Clark's voice cut through the haze, calling men from their blankets while fog curled along the riverbanks. The daily routine was no lazy drift. The camp broke with practiced efficiency—fires doused, tents folded, gear repacked in darkness. Some men fetched water for parched kettles, others checked gunpowder flasks, and patched worn moccasins.

You might find yourself hauling heavy barrels from shore to boat, hands numb, sweat already gathering despite the chill. The labor was relentless, and everyone had a role: some rowed; others managed supplies; a few, trusted with navigation, studied the river's twists for hidden threats or the best channel.

The heart of their adventure was the keelboat—a floating lifeline that doubled as home, warehouse, and fortress. This boat stretched nearly fifty-five feet, its broad beam packed with barrels, crates, and trunks. Down the center ran a narrow passage for walking, but most space was given to storage: food, gunpowder, trade goods, scientific tools. The crew slept above the cargo where they could grab their rifles at a moment's notice; hammocks swung between ribs or bedrolls unrolled atop planks.

Clark and Lewis had a small covered cabin in the stern—barely more than a box—where they wrote journals and sketched maps by candlelight. On deck, two brass swivel guns glinted in sunlight, ready to repel an ambush or signal for help. Every item had its place—if you stowed gear wrong, you risked losing it all at the next sharp bend.

Alongside the main boat traveled two pirogues—long, open crafts that were fast but risky in rough water. The "white pirogue" carried delicate supplies—flour, medicines, and trade goods—while the "red pirogue" often hauled heavier cargo and served as backup if disaster struck. The pirogues needed lighter hands and quick reflexes; they could dart through shallows or slip between snags where the keelboat dared not go. Crewmen rotated between vessels, sharing both risk and responsibility. On wide stretches, they hoisted canvas sails to catch any friendly wind—but more often, you'd see men grimacing as they pushed long poles against muddy bottoms or strained at oars for hours.

River navigation was never simple. The Missouri was a wild thing—full of shifting sandbars and tangling snags that could flip a boat in seconds. One day you might make twenty miles; another day you'd fight just to keep from going backward. Sometimes men leapt overboard to heave on ropes and drag vessels past obstacles.

A submerged cottonwood could rip a hole in your hull or toss all your goods into swirling water. Each day brought fresh trouble: a half-sunken log scraping the side at dawn, a sandbar trapping you until dusk. At times, panic took over when cargo shifted too far, or a sudden current threatened to capsize everything. Lewis wrote of "constant labor and apprehension," recording near-misses and lost provisions with a kind of grim pride.

The crew's methods for moving upriver changed with every mile. When the current ran slow, oarsmen set a steady pace, backs hunched to their work. In stronger flow or shallow water, men used long poles called "setting poles"—one end pressed into the riverbed, the other braced against their shoulders as they marched from bow to stern. If the wind allowed, sails unfurled, though gusts could send you crashing sideways if not handled right. Sometimes ropes snaked ashore, and teams hauled with brute force from muddy banks—one slip meant disaster for all.

Even with so much danger and exhaustion, life on board was not without its lighter moments. When dusk settled over camp, and fires crackled near shore, stories flowed as freely as whiskey rations allowed. Men shared tales of home or swapped jokes about the day's blunders: a spilled sack of flour, Clark's dog Seaman chasing raccoons through sleeping quarters. Fiddlers played lively tunes; voices rose in song to drown out fear or fatigue. Yet discipline was strict; rules kept chaos at bay when tempers flared, or mistakes threatened safety. Lewis and Clark did not hesitate to hold "court-martials"—formal trials for insubordination or theft. Punishments ranged from extra duties to lashes on bare backs. Most learned quickly that teamwork mattered more than pride.

Facing the Elements – Weather, Wildlife, and River Hazards

Thunder boomed across the river valley and brought everything to a halt. The Missouri could turn violent in an instant. One moment, the sky was bright; the next, it was a churning wall of gray, rain pelting down with a force that soaked every blanket and swept mud over every dry patch of ground. The men huddled under makeshift tarps or pressed close to the hull, shivering as wind howled through clothes already battered by days of sun. When the storm passed, the air hung heavy and wet, while the sun returned with a vengeance, baking the deck until it was almost too hot to walk barefoot. Sweltering afternoons left you dizzy and searching desperately for shade that rarely appeared along the open banks. Nights could be equally cruel, especially as late spring gave way to early summer.

Cold crept in as fog rolled off the river, making sleep a restless affair. Morale swung with the weather—some mornings everyone joked through adversity, but other days tempers flared and exhaustion set in. Clark described one storm as "violent and incessant," his pen scratching out complaints about "the intolerable weather" that stopped progress for hours or even days. Nature's unpredictability didn't stop with the sky. Every time you thought the expedition had settled into a rhythm, Missouri wildlife reminded you how new and raw this land truly was.

The riverbanks were alive with beavers slapping their tails at dusk and deer feeding in tall grass nearby. Waterfowl rose in sudden clouds at sunrise—geese, ducks, herons—all filling the air with their wild noise. The sight of these animals was more than a spectacle; it meant food for hungry bellies and furs for barter, but it also brought its own set of problems. Swarms of mosquitoes descended at dusk and dawn, biting through shirts and even blankets. Journals filled with complaints about "clouds of tormenting insects" that left faces swollen and eyes watering. If you were unlucky, biting flies joined in, targeting ankles and hands until every task felt like punishment.

Not all animals were easily managed. Early in their progress upriver, Lewis recorded seeing enormous bear tracks in soft mud near the shore—evidence of grizzlies. Nobody in the Corps had faced these creatures before. Local legends described them as unstoppable, and soon enough, there were real encounters. The first time a bear charged from the willows, it scattered men in every direction. Rifles jammed, powder wouldn't light fast enough, and only desperate firing drove the animal away. Afterward, new rules emerged: never leave camp alone, always keep weapons dry and within reach. Men who once laughed at such stories now checked over their shoulders any time they saw fresh tracks.

The river itself never let anyone forget that disaster lurked just beneath the surface. Submerged logs—called "sawyers" because they bobbed up and down like a saw—could rip a hole in your boat when least expected. Sometimes they'd look safe from above, but snagged ropes or broke oars with a sudden jerk. Navigating around these hazards took constant vigilance; you learned to read small ripples or listen for the thud of wood against hull. No one could relax completely, not even for a moment. Men rotated through lookout duty, calling out warnings or signaling for quick changes in course.

Accidents happened despite every precaution. A slip on wet planks sent men overboard into water cold enough to shock breath from lungs. Sometimes a rope snapped under strain, sending a crewman sprawling or pinning fingers between heavy cargo and the deck rail. Injuries ranged from gashed hands to twisted ankles or worse. When someone fell in, shouts rang out, and everyone scrambled—some tossed lines while others grabbed poles to pull the unlucky man back before the current swept him away.

Lewis's frustration with these setbacks spilled onto the pages of his journal. He wrote about "slow progress" and "endless impediments," his words edged with disappointment but also stubborn determination. Clark often tried to soften these blows by focusing on what they learned each day, yet even he sometimes confessed that storms or mishaps "much retarded our advancement." These records show not just facts but emotion—fatigue, annoyance, small victories snatched from the jaws of disaster.

If you've ever spent time outdoors in unpredictable weather or dealt with swarms of biting insects, you might understand a fraction of what the Corps endured day after day. They battled not just distance but an environment that fought back at every turn—weather that could upend plans in an instant, wildlife that alternated between friend and foe, a river more obstacle than highway most days. Every mile was paid for in sweat, bites, bruises, and sleepless nights, yet still they pressed on—hungry for discovery but always mindful that nature set every rule along this wild stretch of water.

York's Journey – The Role and Reality of Enslavement

York's story stands out like a ripple on the surface of the Missouri—always present, changing shape as the days wore on. If you watched him in camp, you would see a man built for labor, his broad shoulders moving crates or hauling water while others paused to catch their breath. York's physical might was legendary among the Corps. He could outlast most men at the oars, and when hunting was slow, his tracking skills and steady aim often meant the difference between an empty pot and a hearty meal. His role stretched from heavy lifting to essential camp chores, and no one doubted his value when work needed doing. Yet, while York shared in every hardship, he did so from a position no other man in the Corps experienced—he was Clark's enslaved servant, never free to make choices the others took for granted.

You might imagine the camp as a place where everyone stood equal, but power shaped every interaction. Clark could order York to labor long after others had retired for the night. The other members respected York's strength, sometimes even joking or gambling with him, but the boundary between camaraderie and command was never erased. When the Corps voted on important matters later in the expedition, York's voice counted—an astonishing break from the rules of society at that time—but he still slept at Clark's feet, fetched his meals, and waited for orders each morning. Some moments reflected genuine respect: men cheered York's feats in wrestling or admired his skills with horse and rifle. Yet other times, he was left on the margins, not included in planning or given the same rations during lean weeks.

York's experience was shaped by contradiction. He was indispensable but never independent. In private, he bore the brunt of Clark's frustrations and sometimes served as a buffer when other men broke rules—Clark disciplined York harshly for perceived slights or failures that would have drawn less attention if committed by others. These were small reminders of his lack of agency, woven into daily life. At the same time, no one could ignore his contributions. He carried double loads without complaint, broke trails through tangled brush, and calmed tempers at firesides when storms or hunger left nerves raw.

Encounters with Native nations brought another layer to York's reality. For many Indigenous people along the Missouri, York was their first close look at a Black man. Children and elders alike stared in awe; some reached out to touch his skin or hair, curious about this stranger so different from themselves and the white members of the Corps. Stories spread quickly—some called him "Big Medicine" or believed he held special powers. During formal meetings with tribal leaders, Clark sometimes encouraged York to display his strength or dance. These performances were uncomfortable reminders of his lack of control over how he was seen. Yet, they also gave him visibility; in some councils, Native leaders showed more interest in York than in Lewis or Clark, asking questions and offering gifts.

Journal entries from Clark, Lewis, and others capture these moments with a mix of fascination and awkwardness. One describes how a group of Arikara elders watched York with "great wonder," another how Sioux children followed him everywhere he went, laughing and mimicking his movements.

In some accounts, York himself played along—twirling in mock dances or flexing muscles to amuse his audience. But these glimpses are always filtered through someone else's pen. We never hear York's own words, his thoughts about being both visible and voiceless.

When you look closer at York's agency, you find it is both present and painfully limited. He made requests for time off to visit with friendly Native groups or to fish alone, small freedoms won through trust and necessity rather than right. After the expedition returned east, York asked Clark for his freedom—pointing to all he had done for the Corps, all he had risked and achieved alongside free men.

His requests were first denied; Clark believed he owed obedience for life despite everything they had shared on the trail. Historians still debate what happened next: some accounts say York was eventually freed years later; others say he died still enslaved or disappeared into obscurity. What is certain is that York's story never found its way into his own hand—the journals that survive describe him but never let him speak for himself.

The absence of York's voice is a silence that echoes through every retelling of these events. It is easy to admire his grit, but harder to sit with what he endured: celebrated as a peer some days, treated as property on others, always subject to the choices of someone else. That tension gives York's legacy both its weight and its ache—a reminder that discovery is never simple, that real people carried its burdens in ways history often forgets.

First Councils – Diplomacy with the Oto and Omaha Nations

You can almost picture the tension hanging in the air as the Corps of Discovery prepared for its first formal meetings with Native leaders. No one in the boats missed the shift from grunt work to a kind of military theater. Shirts were scrubbed, boots polished, brass buttons shone until they caught the sun. Flags unfurled over the camp in a bold statement. Lewis and Clark understood that appearances mattered. They called the men to stand in line, muskets at their sides, forming ranks along the riverbank. Drums rolled. The American flag—new to many onlookers—fluttered above the parade, signaling both welcome and warning. These displays weren't just for show. They were calculated moves meant to impress, but also to communicate strength and intent even before a word was spoken.

The first council with the Oto, and then later the Omaha, unfolded like a ceremony written with anxiety and hope. The leaders of these nations approached with their own sense of gravity, wearing robes of buffalo hide, faces painted with ochre or charcoal. Each side brought gifts, but the meanings behind them couldn't have been more different.

Lewis and Clark carried peace medals stamped with President Jefferson's likeness—heavy silver coins meant to symbolize friendship but also U.S. authority. They offered bolts of cloth, mirrors, beads, knives, and tobacco, hoping to win favor or at least curiosity. These items were laid out on a blanket as if on an altar, each piece placed deliberately.

Council meetings themselves followed a carefully rehearsed script. The Corps sat in semicircles around a fire or inside a large tent. Lewis would rise, chest tight with nerves, and read aloud a speech from Jefferson. The words had been written far away in Washington, describing the

United States as a "great father" and promising peace, protection, and trade in exchange for loyalty. The speech was then filtered—sometimes through two or three interpreters—into French, then into the Oto or Omaha language.

If neither party shared enough vocabulary, sign language filled the gaps: hands slicing through air to describe rivers, trees, or kinship ties. Every pause stretched long as meanings shifted between worlds. Sometimes a phrase that seemed simple in English became tangled or even threatening in translation.

Native leaders listened with watchful eyes and measured answers. Some were openly skeptical—why should they trust these newcomers with their bright buttons and strange flags? They asked questions about trade goods: Would the Americans bring guns, ammunition, and iron tools? Would they protect villages from rival tribes or simply pass through? More than once, chiefs stood to assert their own sovereignty, reminding Lewis and Clark that they spoke for powerful nations with long histories of alliance and rivalry.

They requested proof that this new "father" in Washington would honor promises better than previous traders or far-off officials. Negotiation was never one-sided. Oto and Omaha leaders pressed for practical benefits: access to trade routes, fair prices for pelts and horses, perhaps help against enemies from up or downstream. Some insisted on gifts before talking further; others used silence as their sharpest tool.

For every medal received and handshake exchanged, there was an unspoken calculation—how much trust to give, how much to hold back. The Americans sometimes missed these subtle cues, confusing patience for agreement or assuming that a council ended with mutual understanding when it often did not.

Early results were mixed at best. The first exchanges were marked by misunderstandings on both sides. At one council, an Oto chief accepted Jefferson's medal but later asked pointedly how many Americans would come next year—and whether their arrival meant war or peace. Lewis worried in his journal about "communication difficulties," noting that some chiefs seemed offended by certain requests or promises. Clark grumbled privately that progress was slow, frustrated by what he saw as delays or evasions.

The Corps quickly realized they needed to adapt. Rehearsed speeches gave way to more listening and more questions about local customs and needs. They learned to bring extra trade goods and to let interpreters take their time rather than rushing talks. Flags became less about dominance and more about signaling openness to further conversation. These lessons shaped every future council up the river—and left permanent marks on how Americans would try (and often fail) to build trust on new ground.

Journal entries from these first councils are filled with sharp details: descriptions of painted faces watching every move; sketches of ceremonial pipes passed from hand to hand; notations of awkward silences when meaning slipped out of reach. The records show not just facts but confusion, hope, and humility—a recognition that real diplomacy meant learning as much as leading. In those moments by the fire, history turned on gestures as much as on words, revealing how much of discovery is about listening as well as speaking.

Journaling the Journey – Recording New Lands and Experiences

Every night, after the campfire flickered low and most men settled into their blankets, a few figures hunched over battered field desks. These were sacred moments for Lewis and Clark. The ritual of writing down what had happened, what had been seen, felt almost like a promise—to memory, to science, to whoever would read their words in years to come. Lewis approached his journal with a scientist's eye. He described plants in careful detail, noting the shape of leaves, the color of flowers, and the way a stem bent in the wind.

He watched animals—sometimes for hours—recording how a beaver gnawed through willow, or how a strange bird swooped in morning mist. His words chased accuracy, sometimes bordering on obsession. Clark, though, looked at the land with a different set of priorities. He made sure to mark every twist and fork of the river, every sandbar that might wreck a boat.

His pages were filled with distances and bearings, sketches of bluffs and islands, notes on where fresh water could be found or where the bank threatened to give way beneath a careless step. Writing wasn't easy. Most days ended with exhaustion so deep it felt like an ache in the bones. Rain turned ink to watery streaks, splattering pages with mud or silt. More than once, a gust whipped away loose sheets— sometimes lost forever in the current. Lewis and Clark struggled with ink that clumped or froze; they experimented, trying homemade blends from lampblack and honey or crushed berries when supplies ran low. They carried their papers in oilskin pouches, tightly wrapped to guard against rain or an accidental dunking in the Missouri. Even so, stains and smudges crept in, evidence of rough living. Sometimes entries stopped mid-sentence—a thunderstorm too fierce, an animal alarm too urgent to ignore.

These problems didn't stop them from documenting everything they could. Lewis wrote on May 16th about "the boundless prairie stretching out before us, as green as any sea." He described antelope bounding out of reach, prairie dogs vanishing into burrows at the sound of footsteps. Clark sketched a map of a meandering creek lined with cottonwoods—each bend carefully measured with compass and pace. He captured the outline of a distant bluff, labeling it with names chosen on the spot. Their journals weren't just lists of facts.

They pulsed with first impressions: awe at endless grasslands waving under the wind; confusion at the tangled chatter of languages drifting from Native villages across the water. There were entries about the bright yellow sunflowers growing wild along muddy banks and about bison herds so vast that they blocked any view ahead.

Mood found its way into these pages, too. Lewis sometimes wrote of "melancholy," especially on days when progress lagged, or tempers frayed. Clark's tone swung between determination and weariness; he confessed to feeling "dispirited" after days when rain halted them for hours on end or when sickness swept through camp.

Still, there were moments of excitement—a new animal spotted, a successful crossing recorded with pride. The journals became not just records but companions. On lonely nights, writing gave shape to worry or hope. These writings served a dual purpose from the start. Lewis knew Jefferson expected more than tall tales; the president wanted proof— real data that could change maps and fill books back east.

Every botanical sketch, every charted river bend was meant for eventual publication. The plan was bold: these raw notes would become a public record, a testament to what had been accomplished, and a guide for those who would follow. Lewis and Clark dreamed that their journals would help build new knowledge—about nature, geography, even medicine—and show Americans what was possible far beyond the horizon.

But there was something more personal at work, too. Writing forced both men to reflect on their own choices— why they pushed forward despite all odds, what it meant to see so much newness each day, how the people around them shaped every discovery and setback. Their journals became mirrors as much as windows; through them, we can almost step into their minds and share what they saw and felt.

Early sketches scattered through the pages show how seriously they took this task. Lewis drew careful diagrams of flowers and animal tracks; Clark's maps bristle with notations about hazards and safe harbors. Even when lines wavered, or ink ran thin, their intention never faltered: preserve this experience for others—scientists, politicians, dreamers—who might need these truths one day.

Crossing Paths – Early Clashes and Cooperation with the Sioux

As the Corps pressed farther into the heart of the Missouri, word spread ahead of them. The land they entered was controlled by powerful nations—the Sioux, divided into branches like the Yankton and the formidable Teton. These were not isolated villages but expansive societies that shaped the flow of trade and the balance of power across vast distances.

The Sioux dominated the river's commerce, holding sway over furs, horses, and alliances. Their reputation was more than rumor; it was built on generations of negotiation and force. When you moved through this territory, you did so with a sense of both awe and wariness, knowing that each bend in the river might bring a meeting—welcome or otherwise.

The first encounters felt charged with uncertainty. The Corps approached Sioux lands with gifts and formal greetings, expecting to follow patterns set with other nations. But Teton Sioux leaders—accustomed to being gatekeepers along this stretch—demanded more than tokens of friendship. They insisted on tribute for safe passage, openly asking for whiskey, tobacco, and other goods. Their warriors lined the banks, painted and armed, making their numbers clear. At one tense landing, a Teton chief grabbed the rope of a Corps boat, refusing to let go until his demands were met. This was not just about trade; it was a display of power, a test to see if these newcomers understood who truly ruled this river.

Lewis and Clark recognized the stakes instantly. They responded by parading their own strength—lining up soldiers in formation, displaying muskets and swivel guns from the deck, making it obvious that they would not be bullied. Yet, beneath the surface, anxiety simmered. Each side tried to read the other's intentions in small gestures: how quickly hands moved to weapons, how long an offer of tobacco was refused before being accepted. Misunderstandings multiplied. The Americans spoke often of "peace" and "friendship," but these words fell flat when paired with shows of force. The Sioux leaders saw bluster and read caution as weakness or disrespect.

One afternoon stands out in the records—a near catastrophe on the riverbank when a standoff escalated. Voices rose. Hands hovered near triggers. Lewis wrote of "the most anxious moment" he had faced so far, his mind racing through possible outcomes as muskets bristled on both sides. For a few minutes, it seemed a single misstep would lead to violence no one could control.

The Americans believed their mission was one of discovery and diplomacy; the Sioux saw it as an intrusion into established order. Both sides misunderstood each other's signals—gifts mistaken for bribes, warnings disguised as smiles. The journals from these days reveal different perspectives: Clark's terse accounts filled with frustration at "insolence," Lewis's more anxious notes about needing "to avoid bloodshed if possible." Yet even now, you can sense their respect for Sioux resolve.

Despite these tensions, moments of cooperation did emerge. There were evenings when both camps sat together around fires, sharing pipes and stories in halting language. Meals were exchanged—dried buffalo for biscuits, tobacco for corn. Sometimes laughter broke out when gestures replaced words. On one memorable night, a peace pipe passed from hand to hand while both sides watched the smoke curl into darkness, everyone aware that this fragile calm could vanish at dawn.

Over time, the Corps managed to negotiate passage—a victory less of dominance than persistence and luck. They left behind gifts but also questions about what would come next as more Americans moved upriver. Lewis noted that "every tribe must be met on its own terms," and Clark grudgingly admired the Sioux's ability to hold their ground.

These early encounters with the Sioux highlight a pattern that would repeat again and again: hope for friendship balanced against fear of conflict, brief understanding shadowed by deep-seated mistrust. The Corps learned that crossing this land meant navigating not just rivers but relationships—each one shaped by centuries of history they could only begin to grasp.

As this chapter closes, I want you to remember how fragile progress felt in these moments—how easily a handshake could become a standoff and how cooperation sometimes sprang from places you least expected. These early tests along the Missouri set the stage for even greater challenges ahead as winter approached and new alliances formed on open plains and wooded bluffs.

Chapter 3: Winter Among the Mandan – Survival, Diplomacy, and Discovery

Building Fort Mandan – Shelter on Frozen Ground

The first real bite of Dakota winter caught you off guard. One morning, you woke to ice crusting the river, your breath hanging like smoke in the dawn. The air was sharp as a knife, and the sun seemed tired, barely rising above the horizon. The makeshift tents and canvas shelters that had gotten you this far suddenly felt as fragile as paper. You knew—everyone knew—that without a proper fort, you wouldn't last long in this kind of cold. The Corps had to act fast, and every step was heavy with the urgency of survival.

Lewis and Clark didn't choose the site for Fort Mandan by accident. They scouted the banks below the Mandan villages, searching for a place close enough to trade and communicate with their hosts but far enough to defend against any threat. The spot they picked sat on a gentle rise above the floodplain, its back guarded by a thick stand of cottonwoods. Those trees became lifelines. With axes ringing through the crisp air, men set to work felling timber, stripping bark, and hauling logs by hand and sled. The ground was already hardening, so digging for posts and foundations meant hacking through frost, sometimes with numb fingers that barely felt the tools. You could hear the river groaning under the first layers of ice as each log thudded into place.

The design of Fort Mandan came out of necessity more than style. Clark sketched out plans for a triangle-shaped stockade, each side anchored by a sturdy blockhouse—part living space, part lookout tower. The palisade walls rose sixteen feet high, sharpened at the top for defense. Every log had to fit snugly; there was no room for gaps that would let in snow or a darting arrow. Inside the walls, the men built bunkhouses for sleeping, storerooms for food and powder, and a few small rooms for officers. No detail was wasted— scraps of timber became benches, pegs for hanging coats or weapons, even makeshift shutters for windows.

The daily routine was relentless: carpenters measured and sawed; strong backs heaved logs into place; guards kept watch for any sign of trouble; cooks built fires and tried to stretch supplies with whatever they could find or trade.

Building Fort Mandan wasn't just about putting up walls— it shaped every part of daily life. Clark directed construction while Lewis documented progress in his journal. Each man had a role. The most skilled carpenters handled delicate joinery for doors and hinges; others dug postholes or tamped dirt between logs for insulation. A few were always assigned to stand sentry because you never truly knew what—or who—might appear at the edge of the woods. Even mundane jobs mattered: someone always had to fetch water from holes chopped in river ice or gather firewood before it was buried under snowdrifts.

The fort quickly grew into much more than just protection from weather or attack. It became a headquarters—a real home base where maps were drawn, journals safeguarded, and trade goods secured from prying eyes. Lewis stored his scientific specimens in one corner, neatly labeled and packed against the cold. Clark kept his mapmaking tools dry under layers of oiled cloth. The officers' quarters were small but just private enough for planning and writing letters to Jefferson back east. The enlisted men slept in shared bunks—sometimes squeezed shoulder-to-shoulder—but after weeks on the open plains, even cramped beds felt like luxury. There was even space set aside for guests: visiting chiefs or traders could meet by the fire without risking the bitter wind.

Morale shifted almost overnight when the fort's last log thudded into place. You could see it in how people walked—a swagger returned as everyone realized they weren't just surviving; they were thriving, at least for now. That first night inside real walls, laughter echoed off new timbers instead of being swallowed by endless sky. No more waking up soaked or shivering in frozen blankets. The men marked the event with small rituals: a shared meal with extra rations, a bottle of whiskey passed around until cheeks glowed red, even a raucous song or two that drifted out into the dark.

Lewis wrote about it with pride—describing "our comfortable situation" and how spirits were "remarkably elevated." The journals from those days read almost like celebrations; after so many miles and so much uncertainty, they had built something solid in a world that often felt anything but.

The Mandan and Hidatsa – Allies, Diplomats, and Neighbors

When you first looked out over the river's bank and saw the clustered earthlodges of the Mandan and Hidatsa, you couldn't help but feel you were stepping into a civilization built with centuries of wisdom. These were not simple villages but vibrant hubs, their domed lodges gathered close for warmth and protection. Wooden frames, packed with earth and straw, held firm against the prairie wind. You saw children darting between homes, old women shelling corn on woven mats, men mending tools or stretching hides, all beneath the smoke plumes curling from every roof. The Mandan and Hidatsa had chosen this place for its rich soil and its position at the heart of ancient trade routes—a crossroads where river met plain, where news and goods never stopped flowing.

Their gardens, even in winter, hinted at a mastery of agriculture rarely matched: stores of squash, beans, and corn kept hunger at bay when blizzards pressed in. Their location was strategic, tucked where the Knife River joined the Missouri, making their villages a stopping point for traders and travelers from all directions.

Day-to-day life soon blurred the line between guest and neighbor. From the moment you arrived, formal distance melted into practical exchange. Corps members visited Mandan homes to share steaming bowls of corn soup or roasted bison. In turn, Mandan women visited the fort with gifts or invitations to feasts. The air in those gatherings buzzed with curiosity and laughter. Language lessons grew from necessity; you might find yourself repeating Hidatsa words for food or weather, trading English phrases in return.

Children watched wide-eyed as you struggled to pronounce their names. The winter calendar filled with social events—dances marked the full moon, while sacred ceremonies lit up long nights. Corps members received painted faces in ritual or joined in animal-skin drumming circles, learning rhythms that seemed to echo across the frozen ground. Each encounter broke down another barrier. Evenings often ended with stories—some true, some wild—told around fires, with everyone wrapped in buffalo robes and community.

Yet beneath these warm exchanges pulsed a more complicated current—diplomacy that demanded trust but never let go of caution. The Mandan saw opportunity in your presence but expected protection in return. They wanted a buffer against their enemies, especially the Sioux, who raided from the south. You could feel the weight of their expectations every time a chief pulled you aside to ask about American soldiers or guns.

At the same time, Lewis and Clark pressed for information only these locals could offer: details about distant tribes to the west, stories of trails winding through unknown mountains, hints about where rivers forked or vanished into rock. Mandan leaders understood the game—they offered guidance, but guarded secrets that kept them powerful as middlemen in regional trade.

Hidatsa knowledge shaped your plans more than any map from Philadelphia ever could. One winter afternoon, a Hidatsa elder sat beside Clark and sketched in charcoal on a buffalo hide. He drew rivers that flowed north and west, mountains marked by strange symbols, villages marked by dots and animal tracks. His map was alive with detail—places where herds gathered, valleys choked by snow late into spring, trails safe for horses but deadly for strangers.

Watching him work, you realized how much your safety depended on this local wisdom. The Hidatsa explained how to avoid hostile bands, which passes would be open first after thaw, and where to find clean water on a dusty plain. When you asked about routes to reach the Shoshone—crucial for finding horses later on—Mandan and Hidatsa informants laid out options with patient clarity.

Hospitality from these neighbors went beyond food or directions. When one of your men fell ill, Mandan healers arrived with herbal poultices and prayers whispered over feverish heads. Women taught you how to sew fur-lined moccasins that saved frozen feet; children showed safer passages across river ice. After a successful hunt, families welcomed you in for roasted meat and sweet cakes made from dried berries and corn. There were warnings too—stories shared in low voices about sudden blizzards or places where spirits walked after dark.

Sometimes trust wavered. News spread fast when a Corps member offended local customs or when rumors of gun deals circulated at the market. Yet each side needed the other: you hungered for knowledge and shelter; they wanted new goods and reassurance against old threats. Together, you built a relationship that survived not because it was simple or perfect, but because it was necessary through that long and uncertain winter.

Sacagawea's Entrance – Interpreter, Guide, and New Mother

The first time you heard Sacagawea's name among the Corps, it was spoken in a mixture of curiosity and calculation. Her husband, Toussaint Charbonneau, had arrived at Fort Mandan hoping for work as an interpreter. Charbonneau was a French-Canadian trader with a reputation as slippery as the river ice—he had spent years moving between Native villages and fur company outposts, learning enough Hidatsa and Mandan to get by in trade, but never quite settling anywhere. He picked up languages the way others picked up stories, always ready to sell his skills to the highest bidder. Yet Charbonneau alone didn't interest the captains.

What caught their attention was the quiet young woman at his side, Sacagawea. Her story was one of survival—taken as a girl from the Lemhi Shoshone during a raid and absorbed into Hidatsa life near Knife River. She learned to speak both her birth language and that of her captors, adapting to new customs with grace that masked deep resilience.

The Corps' decision to bring Charbonneau into their circle was strategic, not sentimental. Lewis and Clark understood that reaching the Shoshone would be crucial—horses would be needed to cross the western mountains, and only the Shoshone could provide them. Sacagawea's ability to speak Shoshone offered far more value than her husband's faltering French or Hidatsa. The captains weighed Charbonneau's application with skepticism—he was known for his temper and lack of discipline—but his wife's presence tipped the balance. They needed someone who could bridge worlds, and through Sacagawea, Charbonneau gained a place at the table. The agreement was made: Charbonneau would act as interpreter, but it was understood by all that Sacagawea's voice would guide many of the most important exchanges.

Sacagawea's early weeks among the Corps proved her worth again and again. She moved with quiet certainty, pointing out edible roots when supplies ran low or correcting men who misidentified plants along the riverbank. It wasn't just knowledge of food; she recognized landmarks others would have missed—a bend in the river, a break in the hills, subtle cues that meant safety or trouble ahead. Then, in February, she gave birth to her first child, Jean Baptiste.

The timing was remarkable; snow still covered the prairie, and the fort buzzed with anxiety over how a newborn would fare in such conditions. Yet Sacagawea managed both pain and responsibility with composure that impressed soldiers and officers alike. They called the baby Pompy—Clark especially doted on him—and his tiny presence softened even the hardest men. The child became a symbol: a reminder that this mission was not just about maps or trade, but about families, about hope pushing through hardship.

Having an infant in the middle of an expedition changed everything. Nights that once echoed with card games or quiet talk now included a baby's cries. Sacagawea nursed Pompy at dawn before she translated between captains and traders, or scouted for fresh firewood in the snow. She quickly became more than an interpreter—she was a sign to any tribe they met that this company came in peace. Women didn't usually travel with war parties; her presence at camps eased suspicion. Still, expectations piled up on her young shoulders. Most days, she had to balance her son's needs with constant demands for translation, for advice on local customs, for insight into when to press forward or wait out a storm.

The pressure on Sacagawea ran deeper than most realized. She was not only expected to help negotiate with her own people in the future but also to act as a bridge between cultures at every stop. She navigated awkward moments— when men joked harshly or when tribal leaders questioned her motives—without complaint or visible fear. No one recorded how she felt about being pulled between so many worlds at once: Shoshone by birth, Hidatsa by adoption, now an unofficial ambassador for Americans she barely knew.

The records we have come through others' pens—Clark's fond observations about Pompy learning to crawl across buffalo robes or Lewis's lists of plants Sacagawea identified for preservation—but her own words are missing. She left no diary, no letters home, just traces of her choices in the way maps shifted or tempers cooled after tense meetings.

Sacagawea managed all this with extraordinary composure for someone not much older than twenty. She faced bitter cold, wrapped in furs, as she carried Pompy on her back across frozen ground or down slippery riverbanks. Each day brought new challenges: translating between four languages in one conversation, watching over her child while men crowded around asking questions about distant valleys or how best to cross an ice-choked stream.

If she grew tired or frustrated, it never showed in official journals; only hints appear in brief mentions—a "woman weary but steady," a "mother with calm resolve." The absence of her voice is felt as much as anything written about her. Even so, her impact is plain: she turned what could have been an isolated military mission into something more human and hopeful, weaving her quiet strength through every cold dawn and uncertain night that winter at Fort Mandan.

Trade, Gifts, and Peace Medals – Navigating Cross-Cultural Diplomacy

Trade at the Knife and Missouri Rivers was never just about goods—it was a living language. You could hear it in the shuffling of moccasins across frozen earth, in the measured voices haggling over the value of corn or a single string of beads.

Each day, the Corps and their Mandan and Hidatsa neighbors exchanged more than metal food; they swapped expectations, stories, and sometimes even suspicion. Corn, beans, and squash—staples of Mandan survival—were traded for knives, cloth, kettles, or shiny mirrors.

The Mandan children watched wide-eyed as brass buttons changed hands for handfuls of sunflower meal, while elders tested the sharpness of each blade. A little vermilion powder or a blue glass bead could tip a deal, sometimes sealing friendship, sometimes kindling jealousy between families. The economics of these exchanges ran deeper than simple barter; every deal carried hints of status and trust. If you brought out a rare item—a copper kettle or a hatchet with an engraved blade—it might draw a crowd, and with it, whispers about the power or intention of these strangers from the east.

Diplomacy demanded more than trade; it needed symbols. The Jefferson peace medal became the heart of formal negotiation. You watched as Lewis or Clark called together a council, their hands gripping the heavy silver disc stamped with the president's face on one side and a clasped handshake on the other.

With solemn words, they hung these medals around the necks of Mandan chiefs. To American eyes, this gesture marked alliance—a way to say, "We honor you as friends and partners." Yet, to the Mandan, a gift often meant far more: it was recognition of leadership but also a promise—sometimes unspoken—to protect or provide. Alongside medals came bolts of cloth in bright colors, strings of beads that caught the winter light, packets of vermilion for painting faces during ceremonies, and small mirrors that delighted children and adults alike. Every item had its own meaning; a red coat might signal authority, while a knife meant readiness to hunt or defend.

Yet, even as these gifts crossed hands in smoky lodges or open plazas, misunderstandings flickered beneath the surface. Americans expected that a gift sealed loyalty in a way that would last—almost like a contract. For the Mandan and Hidatsa, a gift was part of ongoing negotiation. They might expect something in return days or weeks later—perhaps protection from enemy raids or another round of trade goods to share with their own kin. When those expectations went unmet, disappointment simmered. There were moments when an offered medal or trinket was met with polite smiles but guarded eyes. Sometimes chiefs pressed for more—asking when the Americans would send soldiers to fight the Sioux or bring guns to even old scores. If Lewis or Clark hesitated or gave vague answers, you could sense tension ripple through the room.

Some nights, things went wrong. Once, a misunderstanding over who should receive the largest peace medal nearly derailed an entire council. Two leading men argued over status; voices rose until an elder stepped in to mediate, reminding everyone that gifts could also bring trouble if shared carelessly. In another instance, Clark's attempt to impress with a gun demonstration startled children and left elders unimpressed—they wanted steady exchanges and clear promises, not loud spectacles. There were successes too: after one especially generous trade—three kettles for sacks of corn and dried squash—the Mandan women sang songs of thanks outside the fort walls, their laughter drifting on icy wind.

Interpreters shaped every word exchanged. Sometimes they smoothed rough edges—turning blunt demands into gentle requests or translating confusion into laughter. Other times, they muddied things further. A single mistranslated phrase could shift the meaning from friendly to suspicious. You learned quickly that language was more than vocabulary; it was about tone, gesture, even silence. A nod from Sacagawea or a caution from Charbonneau often decided whether talks would move forward or freeze like the river outside.

American ceremonies sometimes puzzled Mandan and Hidatsa observers. When Clark read speeches about peace and progress by firelight, some listened closely; others seemed distracted or skeptical, perhaps recalling earlier promises made by distant traders who never returned. Yet certain moments truly bridged gaps: shared meals after long negotiations, small tokens passed quietly beneath tables as signs of private understanding. In those times, you felt diplomacy wasn't just about politics—it was about building trust where none had existed before.

Scientific Curiosity – First Specimen Collections and Observations

Winter at Fort Mandan slowed the river but not the Corps' drive for discovery. Even as frost coated the cottonwoods and wind battered the palisade, someone was always out collecting and observing. Lewis, especially, pursued his scientific mission with zeal. Believing every new plant or animal might be unknown in the East, he aimed to deliver more than tales—Jefferson would receive real proof of the upper Missouri's natural world.

The officers and several enlisted men embraced a meticulous daily routine. After breakfast, Lewis often roamed snowy paths, searching for animal tracks or peculiar plants. When a bird landed nearby, or paw prints appeared on the woods' edge, someone would fetch Lewis or attempt to sketch or capture the specimen themselves.

Despite harsh weather, the Corps made a wealth of observations. Some of the most remarkable specimens were animals few Americans knew firsthand. Prairie wolves— now recognized as coyotes—left prints in the slush and sometimes approached the fort at dusk. Lewis described them as sly, fleet, and clever pack hunters. Magpies, bold and raucous, fascinated the Corps; they perched fearlessly and scavenged scrap piles. Herds of pronghorn antelope dashed across the snowy prairie, their speed unmatched. Lewis made efforts to document their movements, describing distinctive horns, markings, and their tendency to vanish in an instant.

Preserving the collected specimens required ingenuity. Lewis improvised as a chemist: boiling bones for shipment, stuffing birds with grass, or salting and folding skins. Small animals were stored in spirits or strong liquor, but when supplies ran low, the men used snow or dried leaves. Each item bore careful notes: "Caught near Mandan village" or "Observed feeding on willow." They wrapped delicate wings with cotton and reinforced bones for transport. Each shipment included letters to Jefferson and lists resembling a naturalist's inventory.

Documenting these finds for an eastern audience called for patience. Knowing that folks in Philadelphia or Washington had never seen coyotes or magpies, Lewis described every detail: fur color, call, diet, and behavior, often including diagrams or sketches. He compared antelopes to deer but highlighted their unique horns and leaping abilities. Comparisons bridged the gap for readers: magpies' curiosity rivaled blue jays; prairie wolves could outwit any farm dog. The aim was to make the plains animals vivid to those who might never see them.

Preparing shipments became a careful ritual. When river ice allowed, a group gathered in the fort storeroom to pack crates by lamplight, layering straw around preserved specimens. Letters were sealed in oilcloth or bladder pouches to guard against moisture. Maps were rolled and tucked into crate hollows. When needed, the Corps used animal hides for padding or sealed containers with local pitch.

This scientific work did not occur in isolation. The Mandan and Hidatsa peoples observed with interest and sometimes amusement as the Corps sorted feathers and roots. Their expertise proved invaluable. Elders pointed out medicinal and edible plants; women demonstrated useful seeds. Native hunters explained animal habits, adding insights only locals possessed, such as seasonal changes in bird arrivals or tricks for discerning predator tracks.

Lewis diligently recorded these lessons, sometimes crediting his sources, at other times noting "as told by a Mandan hunter." He learned about versatile roots used for pain or energy, the ceremonial significance of magpie feathers, and that antelopes sometimes circled back when chased—knowledge that aided the Corps during lean periods. Indigenous science became central to Lewis's entries, enriching not just species descriptions but their roles in daily life and belief.

Fort Mandan stands out for the sheer number and quality of discoveries, and for the blend of new scientific methods with traditional native wisdom. The journals from this time are filled with the excitement of constant discovery—a conviction that staying attentive and listening to those who know the land leads to wonder.

Surviving the Cold – Hardships, Morale, and Daily Life in Winter

When harsh winds swept the prairie, and the Missouri froze, daily life at Fort Mandan became a relentless struggle against the cold that seemed to seep into the bones. Subzero temperatures turned breath into icy crystals, and even buffalo hide layers offered little protection. The river, no longer navigable, became a barrier, isolating the Corps and making routine tasks like gathering firewood risky. Wood supplies dwindled faster than expected; after the best logs burned, men were left scrounging for driftwood or chopping frozen stumps. Often, what passed for firewood was no more than fragile twigs. Rationing became strict, each person receiving a limited share, with anxiety mounting as supplies waned.

Food was another ever-present concern. Dried meat and corn had to stretch further as weeks dragged on, and when hunters returned empty-handed, meals became sparse and simple. Some resorted to chewing softened leather when hunger grew too strong. Food shortage brought not only hunger but also illness. Scurvy lurked, appearing as sore gums and achy joints, while frostbite claimed exposed fingers and toes. Dr. John Shields, a skilled "medical man," improvised remedies with spruce needle or wild root teas to combat scurvy, stitched wounds with whatever thread was available, and used heated knives to treat boils. Lewis and Clark learned local treatments from Mandan healers as well: willow bark poultices, pine resin steams, or snow-packed injuries to numb pain.

Isolation weighed heavily during endless winter nights. Far from home, in a world silenced by snow and wind, the men felt loneliness keenly. Boredom became another trial, as days blurred—chopping wood, fixing gear, tending fires—leaving minds restless and tempers short.

To fight gloom, the Corps found small joys: storytelling around the fire, tall tales punctuated by laughter, dancing on earth floors after supper, and a fiddle carrying familiar tunes. Cards and dice passed idle evenings when fingers weren't too cold to play. Some wrote yearning letters home, their words heavy with longing, while journals revealed an ache for connection—a wish for news or a simple reminder that life outside continued.

Yet hardship also fostered resilience. When gear broke, men repaired boots with spare hide, whittled new handles for axes, or turned broken barrels into stools. Snowshoes were made from willow branches, and every setback became a chance to problem-solve and collaborate, blurring ranks as officers and privates worked side by side. Skills were shared freely—one man's solution became another's lesson. They learned to find humor in failure: a snapped sled runner quickly turned into a story to share over dinner.

The journals from that season show not just complaints, but moments of triumph over despair. Lewis wrote of "the cheerfulness of the men despite severe weather," while Clark remarked that "good humor prevails at table." Even in misery, they found ways to buoy one another—a prank on a sleeping comrade, a shared drink after a hard day, a quiet song by lantern light. These small moments kept hope alive and reminded them that hardship was temporary if faced together.

As winter dragged on, survival became more than staying warm or fed—it meant keeping hope alive while days seemed endless and spring a distant promise. The Corps adapted, inventing solutions and relying on collective strength instead of weakness or fear.

Looking back, that frozen season at Fort Mandan wasn't just about endurance, but transformation: strangers forged into family by adversity. They emerged tougher, more united, and prepared for new challenges as ice retreated and the river signaled the coming of spring.

The winter at Fort Mandan tested every limit—body, mind, and resolve—but also uncovered the Corps' resourcefulness and grit. They survived not just through preparation but by adapting together. With the coming thaw, they faced new challenges with a renewed sense of hope, ready for further adventure and discovery beyond the melting snows.

Congratulations! You've made it this far!

I hope you're enjoying *Across an Untamed Land: The Lewis and Clark Expedition*, and that you continue reading the rest of it…

You may not be aware of it, but reviews are a big deal with both readers and Amazon. Many potential readers like to check out the quality and quantity of reviews that a book has earned, and the better reviews a book gets, the more Amazon prioritizes it on its website.

So, please spend a little bit of time and write a review. All you have to do is locate this book on Amazon and scroll down on the left to where it says "Write a customer review." Then, you'll be asked to rate the book. Following that, you can simply compose your much-appreciated review, be it long or short. A few sentences are fine.

Thanks very much in advance.

Please keep reading,

Blake Whitworth

Chapter 4: Westward Bound – Breaking the Ice and Meeting the Unknown

Farewell to Fort Mandan – Launching into Uncharted Territory

The first true sign of spring was not the sun, but the sound of ice breaking. You could feel it in your bones before you heard it: a new vibration running through the timber walls, then a crack like a musket shot. The Missouri, trapped for months under thick, dull ice, finally gave way. Huge white slabs drifted downstream, piling against the banks and groaning under their own weight. The river changed overnight from a frozen boundary into a wild, charging road westward.

Each morning, you and the others stepped outside Fort Mandan to check the progress. Boots sank into mud where snow had melted, and every man seemed taller—shoulders squared, eyes sweeping the horizon. The promise of movement replaced the monotony of winter.

Anticipation mixed with anxiety, a tension you could taste. The Corps of Discovery moved into a flurry of readiness checks. Oars were inspected for cracks, sails for tears, and cords for fraying. You watched as men inventoried barrels of dried meat and parched corn, counted powder horns and shot pouches, and checked every seam on the boats.

Careful hands bundled journals and precious maps—no one wanted to lose months of work to a careless splash or sudden storm. Sacagawea tested her strength, lifting her son Jean Baptiste and then a heavy pack, while York grinned and hoisted crates that others could barely budge. The river swelled with meltwater, running higher and faster than any remembered from the autumn. Every decision felt sharper and more urgent. The last days inside the fort blurred together with activity and emotion. You packed boats until they groaned under the weight—trunks of scientific tools, barrels of salted pork, sacks packed with beads and trade items, all loaded with practiced precision.

Clark kept watch with his ever-present list, dividing loads so no one vessel risked capsizing in rough water. Lewis checked on the preservation of specimens; each jar of animal remains or pressed flower represented weeks of labor and hope for Jefferson's scientific dreams back east.

Leaving meant more than just closing doors behind you. There were moments set aside for ceremony—no grand speeches, but small rituals that carried their own weight. The Mandan and Hidatsa gathered at the fort's entrance in bright garments, faces painted in patterns that signaled both kinship and farewell. Words passed between leaders, sometimes halting, sometimes flowing—thanks for food shared, warnings about what lay ahead, advice about river forks and dangerous tribes upstream. Gifts exchanged hands: a painted buffalo robe to Lewis; glass beads and copper kettles given to elders; a new knife pressed into the palm of a young boy who had watched the Corps all winter with wide eyes. Sacagawea's relatives embraced her longer than anyone else, knowing she might never return.

As the Corps pushed off from Fort Mandan's muddy shore, you felt an unfamiliar ache—a blend of excitement and loss. The fort faded behind you, swallowed by trees and distance. Now came true vulnerability: maps thinned out, replaced by rumor or blank space; stories about monstrous animals and impassable rapids grew louder as you moved further away from what was known. There were no guarantees from here forward, just the relentless push of water beneath you and sky above.

The psychological impact settled in quickly. You noticed it in the silence that followed laughter, in how men glanced over their shoulders or checked rifles more often than before. Familiar routines vanished; every bend in the river felt like a question without an answer. Some men grew quieter, their confidence worn thin by uncertainty. Others became almost reckless, eager to prove themselves in places nobody had seen before. You realized how much courage depended on knowing where you stood—and how quickly that confidence could unravel when even the land felt alien.

The river itself changed character almost immediately after departure. The current grew faster, twisting around submerged tree trunks and forming sudden whirlpools that tested every bit of your skill at the oars. Islands appeared and disappeared overnight as water levels surged; sandbars shifted without warning, stranding boats or forcing detours that stretched muscles and patience to their limits. Gone were the calm stretches of autumn; now each mile required new vigilance.

Travel strategy had to evolve overnight. Clark began assigning scouts to ride ahead along the banks when possible, searching for signs of game or danger where trees crowded close to the water's edge. Lewis pushed for longer days when weather allowed—sunrise to sunset—with only brief stops for meals or repairs. You learned to pack and unpack camp faster than ever before; tents pitched in twilight were often taken down before dawn's first light even touched them.

The world around you looked different, too—cottonwoods leafed out in green haze, birds calling from branches above ice-cold water running swift and deep. Every sense felt heightened by risk and wonder: smells sharper, colors brighter, sounds carrying further across open prairie or echoing between rising bluffs. Each day brought something new—a different birdcall, a strange animal track in mud, clouds chased across an endless sky.

The Great Falls Challenge – Engineering the Portage

You barely have time to catch your breath as the Missouri narrows and quickens, the banks rising and closing in, when the roar of the Great Falls punches through the air. The sound reaches you before the sight—a thunder that grows louder with each paddle stroke. Mist hangs in the sunlight, swirling above the river like ghosts. Then the full spectacle opens up: water crashes over a series of cliffs, leaping down in layers that stretch as far as you can see. Spray soaks your face, filling your nose with that sharp, mineral scent only a river in full force can create.

The ground shakes with the weight of moving water. Lewis stands transfixed, notebook in hand, trying to find words big enough for what he sees. He's awestruck, scribbling descriptions of white foam and rainbows arching through the mist. He cannot help but measure everything—height, distance, velocity—treating the falls as both a wonder and a puzzle. Clark's reaction runs practical. He scans the cliffs for possible trails, eyes narrowed against glare, already calculating where men and boats might pass. He's less interested in poetry and more in survival.

The realization that there's no way through the falls hits hard. You need to get everything—boats, food, precious scientific gear—around this massive barrier. It is not just one waterfall but five, strung over miles of jagged terrain and split by boulder fields and tangled brush. Clark and his men fan out with compasses and measuring lines, sketching rough maps on scraps of paper and animal hide. They trade ideas in bursts: How far is each drop? Where does solid ground give way to bog? They argue about the best route, then compromise, marking a path that zigzags eighteen miles across uneven prairie and thorny brush.

The real work starts with wagons. You watch as men strip axles from boats, lash together planks with rawhide thongs, and build sledges from green cottonwood. There are no proper wheels—just what can be carved or hammered into place after days of muscle-aching labor. Every item gets wrapped, tied, or hoisted with ropes cut from spare sails. The heat is relentless; your shirt sticks to your back as you bend to lift another barrel or drag another crate through cactus patches. Prickly pear stabs through soles and palms, leaving bloody tracks behind you. It feels endless—days spent hauling, pushing, pulling, sometimes cursing under your breath when a wheel splits or a sledge sinks in mud.

Teamwork becomes more than a word—it is survival itself. You and everyone else must trust each other without question. Someone shoves from behind while another steers; hands pass water skins and patch wounds with torn shirts. No one gets to rest for long.

Even Sacagawea pitches in, her calm, steadying nerves as she wraps bundles or soothes Jean Baptiste through the din and chaos. Lewis obsesses over his scientific tools, packing sextant and chronometer in padded chests, refusing to let them out of sight even for a meal. Clark double-checks every load, barking orders so fast they blur together.

Rawhide ropes stretch until they creak. When they break, someone splices them again with knots learned on other rivers or borrowed from Native guides who shake their heads at such madness. Some men joke about inventing new curses just for this portage; others fall silent, lips cracked from sun and sweat. The prairie offers little shade, only endless grass waving under the wind that dries everything it touches.

You watch as boats are dragged inch by inch overland—sometimes on rollers made from stripped logs, sometimes carried outright when terrain gets too rough. The white pirogue takes the worst beating; its hull groans under every bump and scrape, but somehow it stays together. Precious journals travel wrapped in oilcloths tucked under arms or tied around chests—no one dares risk losing a page of observation to careless handling or river spray.

Through exhaustion and grit, you learn what it means to adapt fast with whatever is at hand. Sledges patched with spare leather, barrels braced with willow branches, even the smallest tool repurposed when needed—all reveal how necessity drives invention. Some nights you collapse beside fires built from driftwood scavenged along the portage trail, hands too tired to untie laces.

Lewis never stops observing. He describes basalt columns rising like organ pipes beside the falls, notes new species flitting through spray at sunset, and sketches wildflowers clinging to cracks in rock no wider than your thumb.

His words mark this place as something more than an obstacle; he sees it as proof that America holds wonders no one back east can imagine. The portage itself becomes a test—a measure of how much you're willing to give for discovery and how far teamwork can carry you when strength runs low.

Encounters with the Crow and the Grizzly – New Tribes, New Dangers

Advancing into vast grasslands and rolling hills, you sensed a change—a restless energy in the air. Soon, the Corps learned that Crow scouts trailed them, their presence more guessed than seen: a fleeting feather, a distant horse's silhouette. Initial contact was subtle, marked by careful gestures and curiosity instead of confrontation. Immediately, the Crow's horsemanship stunned even seasoned frontiersmen. Riders seemed to appear out of nowhere, their ponies agile and swift. Here, horses were everything—freedom, wealth, survival—and the Crow's skill with them set them apart from any tribe you'd met.

Meetings with Crow leaders were calm yet vigilant. Greetings were exchanged, and gifts were exchanged for information. Trinkets, cloth, and mirrors went one way; in return came stories of river bends, distant tribes, and the landscape ahead. The Crow's intelligence—details on trails and hazards—was invaluable. They navigated hospitality and caution with practiced ease. Their quill- and bead-adorned clothing told their own silent stories.

Interpreters, blending multiple languages, helped both sides understand each other. The Crow excelled at observing keenly while revealing little—an art shaped by generations in unpredictable borderlands.

Even as these careful exchanges continued, a new menace grew, impossible to ignore. The legendary grizzly bears described in tales now proved real—and unimaginably formidable. What began as distant sightings quickly became close calls: Lewis shot a bear that he barely noticed before charging him, forcing a desperate reload. Bear encounters triggered chaotic shouts as men scrambled for guns, sometimes firing five or more shots before felling the beast.

Journals filled with anxious notes: "Bear pursued us two miles" or "Rifleballs scarcely slowed him." These were no ordinary bears: taller than a man, with hides thick as bark and claws capable of tearing through leather and bone.

After the first terrifying run-ins, the Corps' routines shifted dramatically. Clark assigned a double guard at dusk and dawn. Fires burned brighter and longer. No one went for water alone; every small errand meant moving in pairs, rifles ready, eyes scanning for movement. Campsites were chosen more cautiously—open ground preferred over thickets, boats secured on open sandbars. Even Sacagawea kept her child close, always alert. The men realized that marksmanship alone didn't ensure safety with such persistent predators.

This new tension changed everything. Campsites were picked for visibility and safety. The journals became more urgent, filled with near escapes—men chased into rivers or up trees, hearts pounding. Lewis once woke to heavy breathing just outside his tent; morning revealed fresh bear tracks circling where men had slept restlessly.

Danger was ever-present, testing the Corps at every turn— bluffs too steep for horses, river crossings muddied by bear prints. Some nights, fear made sleep impossible; other times, it fostered unity as men shared stories of narrow escapes. Morale flagged after injuries or loss of supplies, but also hardened, uniting the group. Leaders became more alert; once-quiet men spoke up during safety discussions and warned others to stay close.

As weeks passed, attitudes within the Corps evolved. The bold grew cautious; the anxious began trusting their instincts. Even Lewis and Clark became more deliberate, listening closely to scouts' warnings and Sacagawea's knowledge of tracks and animals. The unknown became tangible—a real, living presence to be respected, prepared for, and sometimes outwitted, not just faced with bravado.

This heightened vigilance knit the Corps together more deeply than routine ever could. Shared risk built camaraderie; disagreements were resolved quickly when danger was close. The wilderness became less terrifying as you learned to interpret its signs—broken branches, fresh prints—and to rely on each other's senses. Every day was a lesson: about nature's power, about cultural exchange with tribes like the Crow, and about your own abilities tested against the wild.

Charbonneau and Jean Baptiste – Family and Multicultural Dynamics

Charbonneau's place in the Corps was always a bit of a riddle. Some mornings, you'd see him guiding a dugout canoe with practiced hands, his voice wobbly but determined as he called out in French or Hidatsa. On other days, he fumbled with the oars, more a liability than a leader, his nerves unraveling at the first sign of fast water or shifting winds. His reputation among the men was mixed. He could speak several languages, which made him valuable when the Corps met new tribes, but he sometimes misunderstood or mistranslated key words, leaving everyone scrambling to clarify.

Sacagawea, his wife, quietly filled in the gaps, smoothing over his errors with calm explanations or gentle nudges in the right direction. Charbonneau's moments of bravery showed up at odd times—like when he steadied the boat during a sudden squall or negotiated a tricky passage through shallows. Just as often, he provided unexpected comic relief, his clumsy antics and dramatic stories cutting the tension after long days. The men teased him, sometimes with affection, sometimes with impatience, but even his critics admitted that having another interpreter—even a flawed one—could mean the difference between confusion and understanding.

For Sacagawea, every day meant balancing survival and motherhood. Imagine nursing a newborn while navigating miles of river, your arms aching from paddling and your mind racing through mental checklists: feed the baby, secure the cradleboard, keep him warm when icy rain soaks everything.

Jean Baptiste—called "Pompy" by Clark—was more than just the youngest member of the team. He was a living symbol of hope and resilience. Sacagawea carried him on her back or secured him snugly in birchbark baskets lined with fur. Each stop meant finding a safe corner to settle him, calming his cries with soft songs in Shoshone or Hidatsa, and keeping insects off tiny arms and legs. The other members stepped up as well. York would sometimes rock Pompy while Sacagawea ate, and Clark carved small trinkets to entertain him during dull stretches. Men who were rough in battle showed surprising tenderness when the child needed help. The Corps became a makeshift family—everyone invested in the baby's well-being, everyone pitching in.

The presence of an infant changed how the Corps was seen by outsiders. When Native communities spotted Sacagawea and her son among the group, suspicion often softened. No war party traveled with a woman and child at its heart. The Chiefs saw the family as proof that Lewis and Clark came in peace, not as raiders or conquerors. The baby drew smiles from women in villages along the riverbank, who offered food, advice, or amulets for luck.

At one council fire, a tribal elder reached out to bless Pompy's head, murmuring hopes for safe passage and good fortune. On another occasion, a group of children crowded around Sacagawea to touch Pompy's hair and giggle at his round cheeks. These small moments built bridges faster than any speech or gift.

Still, living with so many different backgrounds in one camp brought its own set of challenges and rewards. English rarely ruled alone; French phrases mixed with

Hidatsa jokes, Shoshone proverbs, met sign language gestures, and sometimes all four swirled together in a single conversation. The Corps depended on this jumble of tongues to negotiate for horses, trade for food, or ask directions from passing travelers. Every word mattered—one wrong syllable could provoke confusion or offense. The men learned fast: hand signals became second nature; laughter eased missteps; patience replaced pride when misunderstandings threatened progress.

Sacagawea's quiet authority rose above all these differences. She had lived in several worlds—Shoshone by birth, Hidatsa by adoption, now wife to a French-Canadian trader—and switched between cultures with an ease that left others in awe. Her advice shaped the expedition's route; her warnings about river crossings or unfamiliar plants saved lives more than once. She taught the men how to spot signs of game or where to find roots that warded off hunger. During councils, her voice lent weight to Lewis's questions and Clark's proposals. Sometimes her mere presence—her hands steadying Pompy on her lap—spoke louder than any words.

The multicultural nature of the expedition became both its greatest asset and its constant test. No single custom dominated; every day brought a new negotiation of habits, foods, rituals, and beliefs. Some men grumbled about strange meals or late-night singing in unfamiliar tongues; others found themselves fascinated by stories shared around campfires that stretched back generations. When conflict flared—over chores, over divided rations—it was usually

Sacagawea who stepped between sides with a gentle word or a knowing look that reminded everyone why they were there.

This blend of backgrounds—Black, white, Native, French—created a tapestry more resilient than any single thread alone could provide. It allowed the Corps to adapt quickly to changing circumstances and gave them tools to survive not just the wild land but also each other's quirks and flaws. Jean Baptiste's laughter echoed as a reminder that even in hardship, bonds could form across every border drawn by language or blood.

Star Charting and Navigation – Guiding the Corps by the Night Sky

When night began to settle across the plains, a hush fell over the Corps. Flickers of firelight marked the edge of camp, but beyond that, darkness swallowed everything. Yet, for Lewis, this was when another kind of work started.

You can imagine him stepping away from the low murmur of voices, carrying a battered notebook and a box of strange-looking instruments—his mind as busy as the sky above. Lewis had prepared for this. In Philadelphia, he learned navigation from astronomers and surveyors, mastering tools like the sextant, artificial horizon, and chronometer. These objects weren't just scientific props; they were lifelines in wild country. Every evening, as others tended wounds or mended boots, Lewis and sometimes Clark would set up an observation post—a spot clear of trees with a steady view of the heavens.

Marking latitude and longitude became a ritual. Lewis would steady his sextant, aligning it with the North Star or the rim of the moon. The chronometer ticked nearby, measuring time with remarkable precision for its era. Clark knelt beside him, noting times and angles by lantern. Sometimes, you'd see another man standing ready with a compass, waiting to check their bearings against landmarks glimpsed by day. The process was slow but vital.

If clouds rolled in or wind rattled the tripod, they'd wait hours for another clear window. Sometimes, frustration set in—clock springs wound too tight, ink freezing in the bottle, calculations ruined by a sudden gust or a careless bump in the dark. But when stars broke through, everything snapped into focus: numbers jotted down that would later fix their position on maps no one had yet drawn.

These efforts filled the journals with a new kind of certainty. You could read entries where Lewis described not just what he saw, but where he stood—degrees and minutes north or west, painstakingly calculated from celestial clues. This data mattered more than glory or adventure; it shaped American maps for decades. Each successful reading meant fewer blank spaces and fewer dangerous guesses for those who followed. It's no exaggeration to say that without these nightly rituals, much of what we know about early America's geography would be lost.

Setting up for observations required discipline and patience. The men learned to move quietly around the night's work— no shouting or roughhousing near Lewis's station.

Campfires burned low so light wouldn't ruin their night vision. On clear nights, morale soared—a sky full of stars promised progress and discovery. On cloudy ones, frustration grew as hours passed with nothing to show but damp tents and wasted oil.

Sometimes instruments failed at the worst moments: a dropped sextant lens or a jammed chronometer could ruin an entire evening's work. Lewis improvised repairs with bits of leather and wire, always aware that these tools were irreplaceable until civilization came back into view. On especially tough nights—wind howling or snow swirling—he might jot only rough estimates in his book, promising himself to double-check at the next opportunity.

But then there were moments when everything worked: the air perfectly still, stars sharp as pinpricks above. Lewis would call Clark over to marvel at the clarity—a sky so deep and bright it seemed endless. Sometimes, they saw the Milky Way spill across blackness like a river of powdered glass. On rare nights in the northern country, green curtains of light shimmered overhead—the aurora borealis dancing silently while men below watched in awe. These sights left you feeling small and wide-eyed at the same time.

Scientific ambition drove this nightly work, but wonder kept it alive. Lewis never lost his sense of awe; he wrote about constellations as if describing old friends met on a lonely road. Orion's belt watched over them as they camped by unknown rivers; Cassiopeia's chair marked midnight on long marches westward. Even those who didn't understand the math could feel the magic—how sky and story wove together out in places where no city lights could dim the stars. The Corps' navigation left a legacy far beyond its own story. Each calculation filled in another square on Jefferson's maps, making future travel safer and more reliable for trappers, settlers, and even scientists who would arrive years later.

Sometimes, Lewis stumbled upon "aha" moments—like realizing a certain star rose earlier than expected because they'd traveled further than he thought. These discoveries meant more than just numbers; they told everyone that progress was real, measurable, and undeniable.

On those nights when you looked up and saw ten thousand stars blazing above empty prairie or rocky ridge, it wasn't just beauty you felt—it was connection: to explorers past and future, to people back east waiting for news, to something bigger than any one person could ever hold alone.

The Land Transformed – Plains to Mountains, Flora and Fauna Revealed

Change arrives first as a subtle shift in the air. The endless prairie begins to heave and wrinkle; where grass once stretched forever, distant blue ridges now cut the horizon, growing clearer with every mile. The foothills, clad in pine and aspen, break the long, unbroken line of the plains. The air cools, becomes thinner, and carries the scent of resin instead of sweet grass. Clouds drift lower and race over the mountains; shadows dart across stony slopes. Nights grow colder, and dawn brings pale, mist-filtered light that fades quickly. The team slows their pace, boots scraping over rock instead of pressing into yielding soil. Rivers narrow, their banks squeezed by stone cliffs rather than open fields.

This rising terrain is mapped by its vegetation. Buffalo grass and wild sage are replaced by willows, tangled undergrowth, and stands of juniper and spruce crowding riverbanks. Lewis is constantly at work in his notebook, recording every unfamiliar plant: wildflowers with delicate silken petals, tough new shrubs (some possibly edible), climbing vines scaling the boulders. He gathers samples— pressing leaves, collecting seeds. Occasionally, he finds a dazzling alpine lily or impossibly bright berries. Some roots and shoots, sampled by the men, are nourishing; others are bitter, quickly spat out. Sacagawea points out traditional medicinal herbs, explaining their use in the Shoshone and Hidatsa.

Wildlife keeps pace with the changing land. One day brings the sight of bighorn sheep balanced high on cliffs, muscles taut, horns arcing skyward. Lewis examines them through his spyglass—captivated by their agility. Later, mountain goats with gleaming coats appear, pausing just long enough to lock eyes before vanishing into fog. Tracks and prints bewilder the men: large claws and unfamiliar hooves. After patient tracking, Lewis encounters his first mountain goat, momentarily close before it disappears.

Each new discovery excites the camp. Men cluster around as Lewis sketches, all eager to learn if these animals and plants are known back east, or if they are witnesses to something wholly new. Specimen collecting becomes near-obsessive; jars fill with feathers, bones, preserved insects. Clark helps meticulously label everything so nothing is misplaced. Lewis's notes to President Jefferson glow with wonder and hope that these finds will expand America's understanding of its own continent.

Native expertise proves invaluable. When puzzled by a bitter plant or strange bird, Sacagawea or a guide steps in, offering practical advice—what's edible, what's medicine, what to avoid. Their knowledge often comes with stories: a flower that predicts rain, or animal tracks foretelling snow. This merging of scientific curiosity with Indigenous wisdom guides every choice about foraging and survival.

The climbing terrain grows steadily more demanding. Trails twist into switchbacks, blocked by fallen trees and shifting stones that threaten twisted ankles. Packs seem heavier, air thinner. Hunting is harder—game is elusive among dense forests and rugged ground. The men adapt: moving farther apart, hunting quietly where elk may gather at dusk. Foraging, once a matter of scanning open fields, now involves searching beneath trees or along rocky streambeds.

Camp life also shifts. Broad meadows give way to wedging tents between rocks or on narrow stretches beneath old pines. Fires are smaller but burn hotter, fighting off swiftly dropping temperatures at night.

Emotionally, these days are invigorating. Every new specimen, every animal tracked or plant pressed between pages, raises spirits and renews the sense of adventure. The country's strangeness is no longer a threat, but an invitation. Each discovery hints that the continent is altogether wilder and richer than expected, and every hardship is a step toward unveiling its secrets.

Looking back, this passage is unforgettable not just for its extraordinary beauty but for how it tested—and expanded—the team's endurance, knowledge, and imagination. New sights and experiences were proof, page by page and step by step, of a continent far more complex than any preconceptions.

With mountains rising higher each day and valleys growing colder and deeper, you realize that discovery is about more than new landscapes—it's about seeing how all of it fits together. The next chapter will climb even higher, toward choices that will shape both the expedition and anyone daring to dream of the world beyond.

Congratulations! You've made it this far!

I hope you're enjoying *Across An Untamed Land: The Lewis and Mark Expedition*, and that you continue reading the rest of it…

Many potential readers consider the quality and quantity of reviews a book has earned, and the better the reviews, the more a seller prioritizes it.

All you have to do is locate this book online, scroll down to where it says "Write a customer review," and follow the directions to write a much-appreciated review. It doesn't have to be long. They recommend at least a few sentences.

Thanks much in advance.

Please keep reading,

Blake Whitworth

Chapter 5: Across the Divide – Trials in the Rockies

The Shoshone Encounter – Seeking Horses and Survival

You don't fully realize your vulnerability until you're standing on the edge of the Rockies, burdened only with what you can carry, the landscape stretching endlessly. The river—once your lifeline and supply route—was gone, breaking into streams and barren stone. Every muscle ached from the journey, but the real fear was not physical: without horses, the Corps couldn't hope to cross the mountains.

The maps were unreliable, the peaks endless, and time and supplies dwindled as winter threatened. It became clear: finding the Shoshone soon was crucial, or you'd be stranded in a region indifferent to survival.

Lewis recognized the stakes and sent out scouting parties, shadowlike across the valleys. Each group cautiously searched for any sign—hoofprints, distant smoke, a cold campfire. The danger was twofold: failing to find the Shoshone or stumbling onto hostile bands first. Stories of ambushes and raids haunted the men, making every day tense. Progress was slow; hopes flagged with each day of silence, and even Lewis began to note uncertainty as supplies thinned and conditions worsened.

When a scout finally spotted riders in the distance, the tension was immediate: friends or foes? The Corps approached carefully, preparing to communicate peaceful intentions. Clark donned his uniform; flags went up, weapons were cleaned to signal discipline, not aggression.

Lewis reminded everyone of strict protocols—no sudden moves, voices low. Trade goods were gathered—beads, vermilion powder, mirrors, brass buttons, all chosen to attract goodwill or dispel suspicion.

The first meeting was fraught with suspense. The Shoshone advanced cautiously, horses restless, their gaze both wary and inquisitive. Both groups dismounted, standing their ground. Lewis greeted them openly, hands visible. The Corps set their rifles aside, signaling no threat. Sacagawea's approach was pivotal—not an afterthought, but a bridge. She spoke gently, transforming apprehension into cautious curiosity, her familiar face recognized by Shoshone women.

Relief spread once both sides realized no fight was intended. The Shoshone offered dried roots and water; the Corps reciprocated with gifts and friendly gestures. Rituals played a significant role—food was shared, elders were invited to the fire, and Sacagawea was given space to mediate. Her presence built trust more quickly and deeply than any gift or speech—the Shoshone listened when she explained the Corps' intentions and mission.

Negotiations for horses proved challenging. The Shoshone valued their herds highly, especially with threats from enemy tribes. Lewis and Clark presented their trade goods—knives, cloth, beads, even a musket—each item carefully weighed against the desperate need for horses.

Future alliances and defense against mutual enemies were discussed.

Sacagawea's credibility anchored negotiations; her assurances carried exceptional weight for both sides. The journals from these tense encounters underline the delicacy of the situation. "Gave them a medal with Jefferson's face—explained we wished only peace," Lewis wrote. Another entry captures a moment: a Shoshone girl delighted in her image in a mirror, returning it with a laugh. Gradually, gifts led to horses—a mare at first, then more, as talks progressed and trust grew, enabling the Corps to move their supplies over the daunting pass.

Sacagawea's mediation was essential when misunderstandings or tempers threatened progress.

She clarified promises, translated, and vouched for Lewis and Clark's good intentions, not just immediately but for future dealings. Her involvement was likely the deciding factor—without her, the horses and the expedition's progress might have stalled completely.

Sacagawea's Reunion – Family, Memory, and Diplomacy

Some moments in history are so powerful that they transform everyone involved. When Sacagawea met her long-lost brother, Chief Cameahwait, in Shoshone country, the entire Corps of Discovery was altered. The Corps, tired and anxious upon arrival, had no idea the mood would shift so dramatically. Sacagawea recognized Cameahwait instantly—the lines of his face and his manner took her back to her childhood.

At first, she could hardly believe it. As she stared, searching for the boy she'd lost years ago to war and fate, her breath caught in her throat. Similarly, Cameahwait saw not just a translator but his sister, taken as a girl and assumed gone forever. Years of separation vanished in a moment.

Their embrace was fierce—Sacagawea wept, her shoulders shook, and a stunned silence swept the camp. The intensity moved some Shoshone onlookers to tears, too. The reunion's emotional charge ran deeper than words. For Sacagawea, it was a collision of her past and present, reminding her of everything lost and how far she'd come. For the Corps, witnessing her family reunion broke cultural barriers more thoroughly than any speech or gift could. This was no mere business meeting; it was a family rediscovered against all odds.

Their embrace instantly changed the negotiations, warming relations and transforming tensions into generosity. Cameahwait began treating Lewis and Clark not only as outsiders seeking help, but as guests of his sister. The sense of obligation was now both diplomatic and deeply personal.

This shift affected the Shoshone's view of the Corps. Suspicion and concerns about hidden motives or broken promises softened, replaced by a sense of shared purpose. Cameahwait trusted Sacagawea's explanations, listening closely to her. The trust that formed was rooted not only in negotiation but in blood and memory—the kind that can't be manufactured. Thanks to Sacagawea, the Corps crossed a threshold otherwise impossible.

Her role immediately grew larger. Sacagawea became more than an interpreter: she was now a living symbol of peace, proof that two worlds could meet. When Shoshone elders hesitated to loan horses for the dangerous mountain crossing, Sacagawea pleaded not just as a Corps member but as one of their own. Her appeals, tears, and reminders of family softened hearts. She helped resolve disputes, reassured her people, and convinced them the Americans meant no harm. While the gifts Lewis and Clark offered— knives, beads, medals—were appreciated, they were insignificant compared to the impact of Sacagawea's story.

The Shoshone began viewing the Corps not as unknown invaders but as "Sacagawea's people." This personal connection created a new willingness to share resources. Horses were offered, guides volunteered, and food was shared even during shortages. Sacagawea stood at the center of every conversation; her voice bridged languages and generations.

Yet, this new role was a heavy burden. Sacagawea was pulled between her original family and her new one with the Corps. Her identity grew complex: Shoshone child, captive, survivor, translator, mother, mediator. In one instant, she'd weep with her brother; in the next, she'd translate for Lewis or calm elders' fears. She became the carrier of stories and hopes for both peoples.

Journal entries from the Corps reveal the profound impact of this reunion. Lewis wrote emotionally about "the singular providence" of the siblings' meeting. Clark said it felt as if fortune had smiled on their mission. The Corpsmen noticed negotiations became easier—urgency for horses faded, replaced by shared meals and laughter around the fire.

What resonates most in these accounts is how deeply personal history became entwined with national purpose. Diplomatic success came not only from clever talk or lavish gifts, but from tears shed, memories shared by grown siblings, and trust built gesture by gesture. Sacagawea's reunion with Cameahwait opened more than a path through the mountains—it forged a deeper connection between cultures, showing everyone that real diplomacy depends as much on human feeling as on strategy or agreements.

Crossing the Continental Divide – The Lolo Trail Ordeal

There's nothing romantic about the Continental Divide when you're actually facing it. You feel it in your bones—the air thinner, the sky impossibly wide, the land tilting in two directions. Every step forward means you're leaving one world and entering another. On one side, rivers run toward the Atlantic; on the other, they tumble away toward the Pacific. For the Corps, reaching this line was more than a geographical feat. It was a threshold—one that symbolized breaking free from the known and crossing into what maps only guessed at.

Native guides, especially those who'd walked the Lolo Trail before, spoke of the pass with a kind of reverence and dread. Tales of freezing nights, endless forests, and the thin margin between life and death made even seasoned travelers wary. Their warnings were never dramatic; they just told you to respect the trail or risk vanishing into its silence.

Each day on the Lolo Trail blurred into gray monotony, broken only by sharp flashes of discomfort or fear. You woke to relentless rain, clothes already damp from yesterday's march. The forest pressed close, thick with fir and pine, needles dripping cold water onto your neck. Paths disappeared under brush or fallen limbs.

Sometimes you followed nothing but the memory of a route someone else had taken years before. Climbing was agony for legs already worn thin. The ground tilted so steeply you sometimes crawled, hands numb from gripping slick rocks or roots. Nights brought no relief—fires sputtered in wet wood, smoke stinging tired eyes. Blankets stayed soaked, boots never dried. Sometimes, fog crept through camp, blurring faces into ghostly shapes. The sheer density of trees muffled every sound aside from soft curses or the coughs of sick men.

Food vanished faster than hope. Game grew scarce in those high woods; birds seemed to sense your desperation and vanished at the first snap of a twig. Berries had shriveled or been picked clean by wildlife long before you arrived. You chewed bitter roots, gnawed pine bark when hunger gnawed back harder. The men started to look hollow, cheeks drawn tight over their bones. One by one, bodies faltered—blisters turned to open sores, fevers left men delirious, old wounds reopened in cold dampness.

Horses stumbled more often, sometimes collapsing outright on rocky slopes. You rationed everything—half rations became quarter rations, then sometimes nothing at all until someone managed to trap a squirrel or shoot a scrawny grouse. Clark's journal says it best: "Our situation is truly distressing."

The suffering didn't stop with hunger. Sickness stalked the camp—dysentery from bad water, exhaustion from sleepless nights, sprains and cuts that wouldn't heal in the wet cold. Even simple tasks—like finding dry tinder or bandaging a foot—grew Herculean when hands shook with fatigue. Lewis and Clark argued quietly over whether to push ahead or rest for a day; neither option felt safe.

Sometimes it made sense to leave behind extra gear or even injured animals just to lighten the load. The decision to rest always felt like gambling with your life—stop too long and supplies ran out; push too hard, and someone might not get up again.

Yet it wasn't only bodies that suffered. Spirits began to break down as quickly as boots wore out. Despair crept across faces at dawn when rain started again or when another horse collapsed in the mud. Some men muttered about turning back, voices low enough not to reach Clark but loud enough to infect others with doubt. The risk of mutiny wasn't just talk—it was a real threat as stomachs shrank and nerves frayed.

Leadership became less about orders and more about keeping hope alive, using humor where possible and strict discipline when needed. Clark tried to keep spirits up with stories around cold fires; Lewis kept hands busy sketching maps or writing plans for better days ahead.

The journals from this stretch are raw and honest. Lewis admits to fearing for everyone's lives; Clark writes of walking ahead just to keep moving through his own anxiety. Some men scribbled private notes—simple prayers for strength, lists of things they missed from home, scraps of gratitude for small mercies like a dry patch of ground or a handful of berries unearthed after hours of searching. Despite everything—the hunger, the cold, the exhaustion— most kept moving because stopping meant giving up entirely.

Starvation and Hope – Food Shortages and Creative Solutions

You can almost feel it in your gut: the gnawing ache of hunger that deepens with every step. When the mountains shut out both sun and game, food ran out fast. At first, the men tried to ration what was left—half portions of dried meat, a handful of parched corn, a spoonful of flour. When even that proved too much for their meager stores, they divided what remained into smaller and smaller shares. You might watch a man count out beans, one for each member, then realize there's not enough for tomorrow.

The sense of discipline that held the Corps together began to slip as bodies weakened. Weakness hit first in the legs—men staggered, stumbled, sometimes too dizzy to stand. Next came the loss of discipline: tempers flared, men snapped over small things, and even the strictest rules couldn't keep hunger from clouding judgment. Faces turned hollow, eyes lost their spark, and every new day felt heavier than the last.

Desperation pushes people to try anything. The Corps hunted constantly but found almost nothing—deer and elk had vanished into deeper woods or moved down the mountains. Squirrels, chipmunks, and even birds managed to evade tired hunters. With little luck, men turned to foraging, scouring the forest floor for roots, berries, and pine nuts. Some roots were bitter but edible; others made stomachs cramp or worse. Anyone who stumbled upon a bush with a few shriveled berries felt like they'd found treasure. Pine nuts, tricky to crack and never abundant, became precious.

Some men chewed willow bark just to trick their stomachs for a while. When wild food failed, the Corps made hard choices. Horses had been family to many, but starving men sometimes had no choice but to kill one for meat. The process wasn't quick or celebrated—men averted their eyes as the animal went down, but a stew of tough flesh was better than nothing. Even dogs, companions on this trek across the West, occasionally became dinner. When real food ran out entirely, they tried boiling leather—strips cut from moccasins or belts—hoping to soften it enough to swallow. It filled the gut a little and sometimes kept fainting at bay.

In these grim days, ingenuity became as valuable as any rifle or map. Sharing food was not just polite—it was survival. There were no secret stashes; if someone managed to catch a rabbit or scare up a few roots, it was divided equally.

Sometimes that meant a mouthful each, but no one went without while others ate. The Corps listened closely when Native guides explained which plants wouldn't poison them or how to dig up edible bulbs hidden beneath snow and rock. Even Sacagawea's childhood memories of mountain plants became crucial; her advice led to a few finds that staved off sickness and death.

Yet the lows weren't constant—there were moments when hope flared up unexpectedly. Leadership mattered more than ever in these stretches; Lewis and Clark made a point to keep spirits from shattering completely.

Rituals helped: some men prayed together before sleep or recited stories from home, reminding each other what waited at journey's end. A lucky hunt sometimes changed everything—a single grouse shot by Clark, or a stream thick with small fish discovered by York, brought grins and laughter back around the fire. If someone caught fish after days of nothing but roots, the meal tasted like a feast worthy of kings.

Personal journals from these days capture more than misery—they show flickers of gratitude and faith. Clark scribbled one night about "the mercy of Providence" after they found a patch of wild onions; Lewis recorded his thanks for "a little meat" after days of bitter roots. Men who had no use for religion before now bowed their heads together and said thanks for whatever came their way—sometimes a crust of bread, sometimes only clean water.

These stretches in the Rockies taught everyone what hunger really means—not just empty bellies but minds that drift toward despair if left unchecked. The fight against starvation forced every man to look out for his neighbor as much as himself. Even small victories—a fire started in wet wood, a handful of berries found after hours bent over cold ground—became reasons to keep moving forward. There's a kind of quiet heroism in surviving days with almost nothing but stubbornness and hope, in trusting that something better might be waiting just beyond the next ridge or bend in the trail.

The Nez Perce Lifeline – Friendship and Trust in Crisis

You could see it written all over their bodies—sunken cheeks, eyes hollowed by exhaustion, uniforms hanging from shoulders that had shrunk to the bone. The Corps of Discovery stumbled out of the mountains not as bold explorers but as survivors on the edge. Their boots flapped around swollen, blistered feet, and some of the men could barely keep upright.

Faces gaunt, hands shaking, even Clark—the steady one—seemed less certain. When the Nez Perce first spotted these strangers emerging onto the Weippe Prairie, they saw a group at its weakest, more specter than threat. The air was thick with a nervous energy. Neither side knew what to expect. The Nez Perce had heard stories about outsiders, and these ragged Americans looked desperate enough to do anything. Weapons were set aside in plain sight, but you could feel the tension—one wrong gesture and things could go terribly wrong.

The Nez Perce response was anything but predictable. Instead of suspicion or aggression, they approached with a cautious but open hand. Food was offered—a simple gift that meant everything to the Corps. Camas roots—sweet, earthy, and filling—were passed around, along with strips of dried salmon. Some men nearly wept at that first taste; after weeks of hunger, even a bite of camas felt like a feast. A fire was built, and blankets were shared. Chief Twisted Hair emerged as a calm and steady presence, greeting Lewis and Clark with quiet dignity. But it was an older woman named Watkuweis who tipped the scales toward mercy.

Her story was quietly legendary: she'd once lived among white traders far away and had returned home with stories of kindness she'd received. When some in her tribe argued that these strangers might be dangerous, she insisted that no harm come to them, reminding everyone of the good she'd seen among outsiders. Her words held weight. In that moment, the course of the Corps' fate shifted.

Trust didn't sprout overnight; it grew out of dozens of small gestures. The Corps offered what little they had left—

beads, ribbons, small tools—to show gratitude. Lewis and Clark told stories by the fireside, struggling through sign language and bits of Nez Perce vocabulary they picked up each day. Gifts exchanged hands: a knife here, a painted feather there. Sometimes it was just a smile or a shared joke about the taste of overcooked camas. The Americans tried to repay generosity with whatever skills or objects they could offer—medical help for a sick child, mending an old musket, sharing news from distant lands.

Lewis filled his journal with notes on Nez Perce language, customs, and family life, eager to preserve what he saw as valuable knowledge. Clark sketched diagrams of their homes and described their methods for fishing and preserving food. Both men recognized that this was more than charity; it was mutual respect beginning to take root. The Corps marveled at the Nez Perce's ingenuity—digging camas bulbs with pointed sticks, drying salmon on racks, and weaving baskets tight enough to hold water. In return, the Nez Perce watched these Americans closely, curious about their strange gear and endless questions.

The impact of this alliance reached far beyond those first hungry nights. Chief Twisted Hair agreed to care for the Corps' horses—a gesture that showed enormous trust and commitment. While the men built canoes for the next leg downriver, their horses grazed safely under the Nez Perce's watchful eyes. Lewis and Clark left behind notes, sketches, and promises of friendship that would echo long after they departed.

This encounter created a model for cross-cultural cooperation that stood out even in a time of frequent misunderstanding and violence across the continent. The Nez Perce could have turned away or struck out in fear; instead, they chose empathy. The Corps responded not only with thanks but with attempts—sometimes clumsy, sometimes genuine—to bridge the gap between peoples. They recognized their survival depended on this newfound friendship.

The alliance with the Nez Perce didn't just save lives; it lifted spirits at a moment when hope was nearly spent. Men who had nearly given up found themselves laughing again around Nez Perce fires, learning songs and stories from their hosts. The memory of camas root shared on those chilly evenings stayed with them long after they moved on. When they eventually returned eastward, it was the Nez Perce who handed back their horses in good health—an act almost unheard of in an age when trust was rare and possession often meant power.

What began as an act of mercy turned into one of the most profound partnerships of the entire expedition, shaping how both sides saw not only each other but also what it meant to survive—and thrive—in a wild and unpredictable land.

The Power of Adaptation – Innovation in the Face of Adversity

The mountains quickly made clear that plans meant little. The Corps of Discovery realized this daily as they moved into unknown territory. Necessity demanded new survival methods. With rivers behind and the Rockies ahead, routines broke down. When it was time to travel downriver again, waiting for supplies wasn't an option—they had to build with what was on hand. Pine logs, green and heavy, became dugout canoes. Men unfamiliar with boat carving learned as they went, using whatever tools they had. They burned out the log centers, then scraped and smoothed the charred wood until canoes floated.

It was slow and exhausting. Pine sap stung every wound, smoke drifted through camp, but each canoe felt like a triumph—proof of making do with little and building something strong enough to move forward. Mountain weather required more than muscle—it required imagination.

Cold and snow-soaked clothing, so the Corps repurposed all they had. Shirts became patches for moccasins; hide scraps turned into mittens or hats. When needles broke, new ones were made from fish bones or scavenged wire. Men darned socks by firelight, using thread pulled from worn shirts.

With no stores around, they improvised gun and tool repairs, tying things with rawhide strips or melting bits of lead for new bullets. There was no waiting for perfect solutions; practicality ruled, even if it meant ugly, makeshift fixes.

Adapting meant learning from the land's people. Nez Perce food knowledge became essential—camas roots, dried salmon, and other unfamiliar foods entered the Corps' diet through patient lessons from Nez Perce women. Watching them dig, roast, and dry roots revealed new flavors and nourishment after days of bland rations. Their tightly woven baskets kept supplies dry through rough weather. Local guides' navigation advice saved lives: which streams to trust, which ridges to cross, and how to interpret signs when landmarks were obscured. Each lesson condensed generations of wisdom—a shortcut through centuries of hard-won knowledge.

Leadership had to evolve, too. Military hierarchy alone couldn't handle all the wild new risks. More decisions became group discussions. Campsites, dangerous river crossings—all sparked open debate, stories, and warnings. Votes on strategies were practical, not just fair: no one person could see all the dangers. Shared responsibility became central; the whole group weighed hope against risk, not just Lewis or Clark.

Mutual dependence fundamentally changed people. Strangers became kin, everyone's survival interlinked. Some men unremarkable before stepped up in adversity—a carpenter improvising a sled, a hunter spotting birds in barren trees. Unexpected leaders emerged, finding solutions where others saw only obstacles. Trust deepened through struggle; arguments faded quickly—grudges were a luxury in close quarters.

Certain moments stay etched: when a canoe nearly split on a boulder and men, without hesitation, plunged into icy water to haul it ashore and patch it through the night with pine pitch and hide; or when laughter returned after someone's rabbit fur hat proved warmer than any brought from St. Louis. In those days, the Corps stopped seeing themselves as conquerors or explorers—they survived by gratefulness for every small mercy, every tiny innovation.

Adaptation was less about brilliance and more about stubbornness and humility—a willingness to listen, learn, and let go of pride for the sake of progress. By the last mountain pass, the Corps was transformed: tougher, closely knit, and inventive.

As the chapter ends, one truth stands clear: it wasn't strength but the willingness to change that ensured survival. Adaptation turned hardship into possibility, preparing the Corps for whatever new challenge awaited on the road west, putting every hard lesson from the mountains to the test.

Chapter 6: Reaching the Pacific – Triumph, Trials, and Transformation

"Ocean in View!" – The Moment of Arrival

You can almost hear the wind as you picture it—raw, restless, heavy with salt and coming from a direction no one in the Corps had ever experienced before. For months, the Pacific Ocean was a rumor, a goal so distant it sometimes felt mythical. Now, with every bend of the river, the anticipation was electric. The Corps traded rumors like currency. Some men said you could smell the ocean before you saw it. Others wondered if the water would look different—wilder, bluer, endless. Even Sacagawea, who had traveled farther than most, asked what the sea would be like. Spirits ran high, but nerves frayed. Would it be everything they had dreamed? Or another mirage after so much hardship?

As the group pressed on, the landscape shifted in ways that felt almost surreal. Towering evergreens crowded the banks, their roots tangled in fog and moss. The air thickened with moisture; every breath carried hints of brine and decay. Storm clouds bullied the sky, turning daylight to an eerie twilight. The river itself seemed to widen into infinity, its surface battered by tides and wind. Some days, you could barely make out the far shore. Drizzle soaked through buckskin and wool, chilling everyone to the bone. Yet every step forward was a promise: soon you would see the edge of the known world.

On November 7, 1805, William Clark finally scrawled the words that would echo through time: "Ocian in view! O! the joy." Imagine being there—soaked to the skin, muscles aching from weeks of rowing and hauling canoes, only to look out and see what seemed like an open ocean stretching beyond sight. Clark's excitement burst off the page. But here's where history plays its tricks. You might be surprised to learn that the Corps wasn't quite at the Pacific yet. The great expanse Clark saw was actually an enormous estuary—part river, part sea—still about twenty miles from true ocean waves.

Tides made waves roll up the river, and saltwater mixed with fresh, so it was easy to mistake this place for the open ocean. Still, for men who had faced starvation and storms, this moment mattered more than technicalities. Clark's famous phrase quickly became a symbol of American achievement. "Ocean in view!" signaled not just arrival but possibility—a new chapter for a young nation dreaming westward.

For those in the Corps, this sight unlocked an explosion of emotion. Men cheered, hugged each other, and wept openly. Some fell silent and just watched, taking it all in—the vastness, the promise, and maybe even a little fear. Sacagawea's reaction was quieter but no less powerful. She pointed out familiar plants growing near the shore and told stories of her childhood further west, her gaze wistful as she realized how far she'd come from her people. York grinned and stretched his arms wide; for a man born into bondage, this moment of freedom and achievement must have felt especially sweet. Even Clark and Lewis, usually so focused on logistics and survival, allowed themselves rare moments of pride and relief.

Yet triumph quickly turned complicated. The first waves that crashed near camp were not gentle—they were punishing. Wind howled across the estuary, tossing canoes like toys. Rain fell for days without stopping; everything became slick with mud and misery. Clothing rotted, food spoiled, and shelters leaked no matter how hard the men worked to repair them. It turned out that reaching what seemed like the ocean was only another beginning. The true shoreline lay farther west, hidden behind roaring surf and tangled forest. Some men grew sick from exhaustion or seasickness; others simply stared out at gray water and wondered if they would ever see home again.

The Corps' journals from these days swing between joy and heartbreak with almost dizzying speed. Clark called their spot "Dismal Nitch," a name nobody argued with as storms pinned them in place for days. The initial celebration gave way to a new reality: they weren't finished yet—not by a long shot. They would have to fight through storm after storm just to set foot on solid sand.

Fort Clatsop – Building a New Home in the Rain

After weeks of struggling along the lower Columbia, battered by storms, everyone is soaked, hungry, and desperate for shelter. The urgency to find and build a winter camp becomes clear. Thick forests and tangled undergrowth complicate the search, but the team's priorities are straightforward: dry ground, fresh water, ample trees for building, and proximity to Native villages for trade—yet far enough for some security. Scouting parties pick through ferns, creeks, and mud, returning with hopeful suggestions. Lewis favors a slightly inland bluff above the floodplain, safe from floods and with some wind protection and river access. Clark prefers a spot closer to the game and fish. After debate, the bluff is chosen—high and close enough to the river for water and escape if needed.

Negotiating with local tribes is essential; the Clatsop know every part of their land. Lewis and Clark meet with Clatsop leaders, relying on sign language, bits of Chinook jargon, and gifts. Coboway, a Clatsop leader, listens carefully. After tobacco, beads, and cautious talks, permission to settle is given—though everyone senses this is conditional, to be maintained by ongoing respect and gifts.

Construction starts immediately. Rain is constant—sometimes gentle, mostly relentless. The ground becomes a quagmire. Logs are heavy and slick with moss. Tools rust, axes dull, and saws clog with wet wood. Hands wrinkle from the damp; blankets are sometimes soaked by morning. Fires are hard to keep alive, and dry tinder is scarce. The humidity spoils food: flour sours, meat molds, and hardtack softens.

Despite it all, no one gives up. Teams divide: some fell trees with rain-worn axes, others strip boughs and make pegs for construction. Clark drafts a plan—a rectangle of cabins with a palisade, storerooms at one end, workspaces at another. Lewis manages stores and keeps watch for spoilage or theft. Everyone shares the hardest tasks: digging posts in clay, shaping logs for tight joints, thatching roofs with bark and moss. When nails run out, you use wood pegs; when tar is gone, you seal with pitch or mud.

The fort gradually rises. Living quarters are built first—cramped, but drier—followed by workshops and storerooms. Every section is inspected after the rain for leaks. Repairs never stop. The palisade comes last, providing privacy and a sense of safety from storms and unknown visitors. By December, Fort Clatsop is ready: one big room for meals and meetings, small cabins for sleeping, shelves filled with travel-worn supplies.

Inside, life settles into a monotonous but necessary rhythm. Days blur together: up at dawn under gray skies, bland breakfast, hours of chopping wood or mending clothes, gathering in the evening for quiet chats or cards. The air always smells of wet wool and smoke. There's laughter at first, but it fades as daylight shrinks and hopes for the sun die. Some pass the time by carving or journaling just to break the monotony.

You feel safe, but also confined. The fort protects from the weather and animals, but brings everyone too close. Tempers sometimes flare. Homesickness builds: Lewis writes about missed meals and missed people; Clark vents his frustration at the endless rain and routine. Sacagawea cares for her child by the fire, musing about clear Montana skies. York jokes, but his restlessness grows with each passing week.

Routines work as comfort and curse: morning roll call, shared chores, hunting parties usually empty-handed. Familiar faces greet you at every meal; the same worries repeat—will supplies last, when will the rain end, will anyone remember what you do here? Journals show longing, boredom, flashes of despair—but also stubborn pride in surviving, day after day.

The Chinook and Clatsop – Trade, Tension, and Cultural Exchange

When you finally meet the Chinook and Clatsop along the lower Columbia, you're struck first by their confidence and their style. These aren't isolated villagers; they're seasoned traders, sharp-eyed and quick to grasp opportunity.

Their villages hug the riverbanks and the Pacific edge, built from massive cedar planks, with canoes lined up like a fleet at anchor. You sense right away that commerce is their language, woven into every greeting and gesture. The Chinook, in particular, command respect—a network of trading partners stretches north to Alaska and south along the coast, and their reputation as shrewd bargainers precedes them. Men and women alike wear woven hats shaped like inverted cones, decorated with geometric patterns that reflect both artistry and status. Social rank is clear here: certain families control the best canoes, the most prized salmon fisheries, and the rarest trade goods. Every visitor, including you, is sized up—not just as a guest but as a potential partner or rival.

Within days of settling at the fort, you find yourself deep in negotiations with these neighbors. The Corps is desperate for anything to break the monotony of salted meat—fresh salmon, roots, edible bulbs, even dried berries. The Chinook offer smoked fish, thick pelts of river otter, and intricate baskets; the Clatsop bring woven hats, elk hides, and knowledge of local remedies for coughs or sores. Your own stores are worryingly thin. Blue glass beads—once irresistible—have lost some appeal now that traders have been flooding the region for decades.

Metal tools like knives or kettles still hold value, but you're running short. Sometimes you trade shirts right off your back or offer handkerchiefs or even buttons. When desperation peaks, men offer their last woolen coats or strips of cloth cut from worn blankets. The Chinook rarely gives an inch on price; they know what's rare and what's not. Each trade feels like a contest of wits. One day, you might score a string of dried fish for a handful of beads; another day, a single salmon costs nearly all your remaining tobacco.

It's not just barter—it's a careful dance of expectations and rules that don't always match your own. You were taught that gifts show goodwill or mark an agreement; here, a "gift" can be an opening move in a negotiation or a clever trick to set a higher price next time.

The Chinook have no patience for what they see as stinginess; they expect real value for every item handed over. Property lines are fluid—they might borrow a tool from your supplies and return it days later… or not return it at all.

When you call it theft, they look puzzled. Their sense of hospitality doesn't mean letting guests take whatever they want; it means sharing selectively, showing off prized possessions, then keeping them close. More than once, tempers flare over missing axes or pilfered clothing. You learn to keep an eye on your things during every trade. Some nights you patch up disputes with extra gifts or apologies—other times, you just try to lock things tighter.

Yet for all the friction, real learning happens here, too. The first time you watch a Chinook carver shape a canoe from a single cedar log, it's mesmerizing—the way he reads the grain, splits away slabs with stone adzes, then smooths the hull with burning coals and quick hands. Their boats are graceful but tough, able to ride surf that would swamp your dugouts in seconds. You watch them set nets for salmon at just the right spot on the tide or use simple tools to dig for camas roots in meadows you'd never notice on your own. Some of your men start weaving hats from spruce roots or try out seal oil as a balm for cracked skin. Others copy the way locals layer fur robes over bark capes—strange at first but wonderfully warm in the rain.

Language becomes both a barrier and a bridge. Chinook jargon—an ever-shifting mix of Native dialects and borrowed English words—lets you bargain for most things, though misunderstandings are common and sometimes hilarious. You pick up bits of phrases for "good," "trade," "hungry," and "enough." Rituals slip quietly into daily life: exchanging smoked fish for stories about faraway ships; sharing small feasts where everyone sits cross-legged around a driftwood fire. You listen as elders recount tales of whales washing ashore or distant wars with upriver tribes. At times, you're not sure who's teaching whom.

Once in a while, moments of respect shine through the tension—like when a Clatsop chief lets you handle his prized obsidian blade or when women laugh as they show you how to roast wapato roots on hot stones. There's pride here on both sides: pride in outsmarting rivals at the trading table but also pride in learning something new from a stranger who braved rivers and mountains just to stand in this place by the sea.

Cataloging the Coastal World – New Species and Ethnographies

The rhythm of each day along the Pacific Coast became a study in curiosity and discipline. Lewis rose early, shivering in the damp, notebook in hand, always searching for the next marvel to document. The beach was a living museum—every tide brought something new to examine. Seals barked on distant rocks, their glossy bodies a puzzle for science. Gulls—unlike any seen on the Missouri—

wheeled overhead, their cries sharp and foreign. Driftwood tangled with bright seaweed, bulbous and slick, while strange shells crowded the sand like scattered coins.

Lewis collected everything: feathers, bones, bits of fur, flowers bursting from mossy trunks. Even the smallest crab claw or unfamiliar berry found its way into his growing archive. He called over Clark to inspect a new root or invited Sacagawea to share what she recognized. The men carried pouches and baskets for specimens, returning each evening with pockets bulging and stories to tell around the fire.

Journaling was an anchor in the gray monotony. Lewis's entries grew dense with observations. He detailed the shape of a sea otter's skull, counted the scales of a silver smelt, and pressed delicate ferns between the pages of his field book. Clark, more visual by nature, filled his sketchbook with quick studies—an eagle perched on driftwood, the curve of a Chinook canoe's prow, or the intricate patterns on woven mats.

The journals described furred creatures sliding through kelp beds, sea lions sunning themselves atop basalt rocks, and flocks of shorebirds rising as one against the morning mist.

They noted not just what they saw, but what they heard and smelled: the briny tang of salt air, the constant percussion of rain on leaves, the hiss of waves at high tide. Preserving specimens in this climate tested everyone's inventiveness. The air never seemed dry; mold crept into every crease. Lewis watched helplessly as prized flowers turned to mush within days. Animal skins rotted before they could be shipped east.

Even bones grew soft if left out too long. He tried every trick: drying leaves near smoky fires, packing seeds in glass vials sealed with wax, wrapping feathers in oilcloth scavenged from ruined coats. When containers ran out, he used hollow reeds or carved driftwood boxes. Labels were painstakingly written on scraps of old paper or bark, tied with sinew or twine, so each sample told its own story— species, date found, place gathered. Still, loss was constant. Some days ended with piles of spoiled plants and frustration simmering beneath stoic faces.

The ethnographic work fascinated Clark as much as natural history did Lewis. Every visit to a Chinook or Clatsop village was an education in ingenuity and adaptation. Houses built from split cedar planks rose above muddy ground, their roofs layered tight against the rain. Smoke curled from central hearths where families cooked salmon on open fires. Canoes carved from single trunks lined the banks—sleek, deep-bellied vessels that seemed almost alive when launched into surf. Clark paid close attention to social customs: who sat where at feasts, who wore what during dances, how elders greeted outsiders with formal speeches and gifts. He recorded myths whispered late at night— stories about Thunderbird battles on distant headlands or spirits hidden in fogbanks along the shore.

Language was another frontier. With help from interpreters and patient repetition, Clark wrote down words for "friend," "canoe," "rain," and dozens more in Chinook jargon—a swirling blend of dialects that let traders and strangers talk business up and down the coast.

Art caught his eye: tattoos spiraled down arms and across faces; woven hats and capes told a whole history in their patterns; fish hooks were carved with animal shapes for luck or power. Tools and ornaments—bone needles, abalone pendants, obsidian knives—filled his sketchbook with detail.

Every entry hummed with awe but also humility in the face of so much newness. Lewis confessed in letters that each discovery felt like standing at the edge of a vast library with only a handful of pages deciphered.

His pride in contributing to Jefferson's vision mixed with a sense of how little anyone truly knew about this place or its people. The Pacific shocked and delighted them in equal measure—a world so rich and strange that even after months of study it refused to be fully captured by pen or paint.

Clark sometimes wrote that he felt small here—a visitor trying to grasp cultures whose wisdom ran deeper than any American map could show. Yet there was also satisfaction: knowing that each pressed flower, each page of notes, each careful sketch would become part of a record greater than themselves—a testament to curiosity, persistence, and respect for difference that would ripple out far beyond their own lifetimes.

Winter Hardships – Illness, Low Spirits, and the Will to Endure

Winter pinned you down at Fort Clatsop with a stubbornness that seemed personal. The daylight shrank to a few gray hours, and clouds refused to break for weeks at a stretch. Rain pounded the roof until you learned not to hope for sun. Dampness wormed its way into everything—blankets, boots, even the bread you tried to keep dry by the fire. Mornings, you woke shivering, boots still wet from yesterday, breath hanging in the cold air. The forest around the fort held a kind of silent threat: every log you hauled back for firewood was slick and heavy, and the supply always felt too small for the endless chill.

Clothes never really dried, and even when you wrapped yourself in every layer you owned, the cold found its way through. Fires sputtered and smoked, fighting for life against the saturated air. The scent of mildew and smoke clung to every man, every scrap of clothing, a constant reminder that nothing would be truly dry until spring. As the weeks dragged on, sickness crept in quietly, then dug its claws into the Corps. Coughs echoed through the cramped rooms, starting as a nuisance but soon spreading like wildfire. Some men developed deep chest colds that lingered for weeks; others fought fevers that left them weak and delirious.

It wasn't just coughs and chills. Boils erupted on skin rubbed raw by damp buckskin and wool. Cuts from axes or knives festered, slow to heal in the wet and cold. Everyone dropped weight as salt meat and moldy biscuits failed to fill bellies. Malnutrition made every bug bite, bruise, or scratch worse. Spirits flagged as men realized they were a long way from help—and even farther from home.

When someone fell sick enough to miss their chores, everyone felt the strain. Lewis tried his best with what little medicine they had: a few bottles of laudanum, some bark tea for fevers, and poultices made from whatever roots he could find. Sometimes he dosed men with what he called "thunderclappers"—pills laced with mercury—hoping to shock illness out of them. Most times, the only cure was rest and luck. Once in a while, someone would scare the others by collapsing or babbling nonsense from a fever. The worst cases left everyone quiet and anxious, trading rumors about who was getting better or worse.

The psychological weight pressed down as much as any fever. You could see it in your friends' faces—the way laughter faded after dinner, replaced by silence or short tempers. Monotony gnawed at you: the same routines, the same faces, the same unchanging sky outside narrow windows.

Men talked about family back east, about missed holidays, about good food and dry beds. Homesickness swept through the barracks in waves. Some tried to keep spirits up by telling stories around the fire—tall tales of wild animals or old army exploits. Others organized games with cards or dice, betting with buttons or scraps of tobacco. On days when a birthday or holiday rolled around, you did your best to celebrate: extra rations if possible, a song or two before bed, even makeshift gifts carved out of driftwood or bone.

Still, discipline cracked now and then. Fights broke out over chores or missing supplies; Lewis or Clark had to step in—sometimes with stern words, sometimes with punishment duty. Petty theft became more tempting as food ran low and boredom set in.

What kept most people sane was routine—and leadership that refused to let anyone wallow for too long. Lewis insisted on daily tasks: someone chopped wood; someone else patched leaks; another checked traps for small game. Clark led hunting trips in the rain; even when they returned empty-handed, it gave everyone purpose. Sacagawea mended clothes and told stories from her childhood to anyone who'd listen—her calm was contagious on the worst days. York's jokes and mimicry sparked laughter when gloom threatened to take over completely. Each person found their own small ways to endure: carving wooden spoons, whittling pipes, writing letters no one knew if they'd ever send.

Journals became lifelines—places to vent frustration or hang on to hope. Lewis wrote about dreams of home and spring warmth; Clark listed every sign that winter was breaking, no matter how faint. "We have passed through worse," one entry read, "and will see green leaves again." That stubborn hope moved from page to page, from one man's words to another's heart. Even on the bleakest mornings—when rain drummed so hard on the roof you couldn't hear yourself think—someone always pulled on their boots again, grabbed an axe or a pot or a pen, and got to work.

Decisions and Democracy – Choosing the Return Route

When spring finally started to whisper through the dripping trees, you could feel the tension shift inside Fort Clatsop. The Corps was worn thin—bodies aching, minds restless, hearts set on home. Yet heading east wasn't a simple matter of turning around. Every possible route came with a new set of uncertainties. Lewis and Clark faced a tangle of choices: Should they retrace their footsteps along the Columbia, braving familiar but exhausting hazards? Or should they gamble on new rivers and untested trails, mapping uncharted territory for Jefferson's scientific dream? The need for haste pressed hard—everybody knew that a late start risked floods, starvation, or missing the brief window of good weather in the mountains. But safety was always in the back of their minds. Some men argued for speed, others for caution, still others for the value of discovering what lay beyond old maps.

What set this moment apart was how Lewis and Clark invited input from everyone—not just the officers or the best hunters, but every member of the Corps, regardless of rank, origin, or background. When it came time to decide where to spend the winter and how to tackle the return, Sacagawea and York both had a voice in the vote. This was remarkable, considering the times. Sacagawea, a young

Shoshone woman, and York, an enslaved Black man, were allowed to vote alongside soldiers and officers. Their opinions mattered. This act wasn't just practical; it was a statement. Everyone who had suffered through floods and fever, starvation and fear, was treated as an equal when it counted most.

The Corps knew that every perspective brought something valuable—Sacagawea's knowledge of western geography, York's experience with survival under duress. That night, voices rose in debate and fell into quiet consideration before each person stepped forward to cast their vote on where they should winter. It's easy now to overlook how radical this was—a small democracy growing out of hardship and necessity.

The decision had real consequences. If they stuck to known paths, they could rely on memories and old campsites—maybe even help from tribes who remembered them. But new routes promised new discoveries: rivers unexplored by Americans, mountain passes that might be easier or deadlier than anything before. This wasn't just about maps—it was about relationships. Some routes led through lands of allies like the Nez Perce; others skirted territories where tensions simmered. Every choice could tip the balance between trust and suspicion with Native nations along the way.

The Corps had to weigh not only physical dangers but also how their passage might be seen by those whose land they crossed. In meetings with tribal leaders, gifts were exchanged and promises made—some true, some simply hopeful. The Corps learned that timing mattered just as much as direction; a late crossing could mean snowbound misery or empty game lands when food was already scarce.

Preparations began with equal parts urgency and anxiety as winter released its grip. Boats needed patching—cracks filled with pine pitch or moss, boards checked for leaks. Ropes were twisted anew from whatever fibers hadn't rotted in the damp. Men inventoried supplies: powder horns refilled, flints counted, axes sharpened until they gleamed in the weak sun. They packed away what little remained of their trade goods—beads, threadbare cloths, battered knives—to use as tokens of goodwill or desperate barter on the way home. Farewell gifts were gathered for Clatsop and Chinook friends—small gestures to say thanks or smooth over lingering disputes.

The mood inside the fort swung wildly from excitement to dread. Some men counted days until departure like children counting down to a long-promised treat; others stared at the rain with hollow eyes, dreading what lay ahead. Letters from this period crackle with emotion—Lewis writes of "anxious anticipation," while Clark confides his "apprehensions" about facing swollen rivers and thin game after so harsh a winter. Hopes for reunion with family jostled against memories of friends lost along the way, while fears about survival threatened to drown out every conversation about strategy.

Through all this, you can sense the gravity of choice hanging over every person in that cramped log cabin.

Deciding how to go home wasn't just about picking a line on a map—it was about what kind of people they had become together. The process tied scientific ambition to personal survival and wove democracy into daily life in a way America still struggles to imitate.

As the last snows melted in the forest shadows and birds began calling from wet branches again, packs were hoisted onto sore shoulders, and oars checked for splinters. The Corps was ready—nervous but determined—to face whatever waited east of the mountains.

Chapter 7: The Return – Splitting Paths and Reunions on the Homeward Trail

Dividing the Corps – Lewis North, Clark South

At Traveler's Rest, the Corps gathered around campfires, tinged with anticipation and apprehension. Months surviving the wild had created a tight bond, now tested by the decision to split into two main parties. This was not reckless, but a strategic risk, fulfilling Jefferson's orders to map unknown land, collect scientific data, and deepen American knowledge of the vast Louisiana Territory. Confidence born of hardship—surviving ice, hunger, and danger—was crucial. The group relied on their experience and alliances with Native nations to stay safe.

Every decision was steeped in strategy. Jefferson wanted not only the Corps' safe return but tangible knowledge— new maps, botanical samples, wildlife records, and contact with tribes yet unvisited. The Corps, now seasoned in survival, could cover far more ground by splitting. Lewis would turn north along the Marias River, probing whether American territory could extend to the Canadian border, while Clark headed south to chart the Yellowstone, documenting its route and viability for traders and settlers (Britannica, n.d.). Each route promised discovery and risks—unknown geography, harsh elements, and encounters with unfamiliar tribes.

Logistics mattered. Lewis selected Drouillard for his tracking and interpretation skills, the Field brothers for reliability, and Shannon for his sharp senses. Clark took York and the Charbonneau family, including Sacagawea and her son. Supplies—powder, lead, dried meat, scientific instruments, journals, and gifts—were carefully apportioned. Lewis's party especially carried extra specimen bags and notebooks, while rendezvous points such as the confluence of the Missouri and Yellowstone were established to regroup if plans went awry. Communication relied on both practical strategies and hope.

Clark left messages—carved in trees, left in oilskin bundles—while Lewis told his group to watch for any trace of Clark's party. If trouble struck, these clues could guide rescue or reunification. The plans, reliant on weather, luck, and the hospitality of those they met, sometimes seemed fragile—but it was all the Corps had to count on.

The missions were clear and daunting. Lewis's group would map the Marias, record terrain and mineral details, document new tribes, and collect celestial data for accurate mapping. Clark was to document the Yellowstone's course, gauge its navigability, and maintain discipline among his men—including trusted sergeants Ordway and Gass. Every man's skills were pressed into service: hunting, keeping records, navigating, and ensuring survival.

The moment of splitting felt heavier than previous hardships. Lewis, in his journal, described feeling anxious and resolute. Clark tried to keep spirits up but admitted to concern for his friend's safety. York and Lewis exchanged a silent, firm handshake. Sacagawea held her infant close, her expression unreadable. Jokes about better hunting or faster water soon faded as supplies were checked one last time.

The group made promises—if one party missed the rendezvous by more than a week, they'd circle back to search. Every man understood the uncertainty ahead: unpredictable storms, rivers that could swell overnight, tribes with unknown intentions. Reuben Field, like others, scribbled a quick note to his family and tucked it away—just in case. Lewis's group headed north, Clark's south. Both journeys demanded not just skill and planning, but faith—in themselves, their companions, and the hope that their paths would reunite as promised.

The Blackfeet Confrontation – Diplomacy, Betrayal, and Bloodshed

You might picture the Marias River as a lonely sweep of grass and sky, its waters dark and fast, the land itself holding its breath. Lewis's party moved quietly through this country, every step weighted with the knowledge that they were not just exploring—they were trespassers on land fiercely guarded by the Blackfeet. This northern stretch mattered for more than just a map; Jefferson's vision of America's border reached to this wild edge, and Lewis needed proof of where rivers ran, how far the new nation could claim, and what peoples lived here. The Blackfeet, called Pikuni by their neighbors, had a reputation that made even seasoned traders nervous. Known for their power and pride, they controlled a region where alliances shifted like wind and horses were currency.

When Lewis's group finally encountered a band of young Blackfeet warriors, the moment felt charged with both promise and dread. The initial meeting played out in classic diplomatic fashion—gifts exchanged, hands shaken, signs of peace offered all around. Lewis brought out medals, ribbons, and small tools, hoping to signal goodwill and a desire for friendship. The Blackfeet returned the gesture with tobacco and stories, their eyes never leaving the Americans' faces. Both sides camped together that evening in a clearing by the river. Fires flickered between them as they shared a meal and tried to bridge the gulf of language. Lewis used sign language, bits of French, whatever words he could muster. He spoke of trade, of peace, but also hinted at American plans to arm other tribes—old enemies of the Blackfeet. The tension was real but hidden under smiles and polite gestures.

Night fell with a sense of uneasy calm. Yet beneath the surface, suspicion churned. The Blackfeet had listened closely when Lewis spoke of giving guns to the Shoshone and Nez Perce tribes, who had long battled the Pikuni for horses, hunting grounds, and honor. For the Blackfeet, this was more than an insult; it was a threat to their power and way of life. As darkness deepened, two worlds shared a fireside but not trust. The Americans drifted off to uneasy sleep while their guests exchanged quiet glances.

Before dawn broke, everything changed. Joseph Fields woke to the sound of soft footsteps and caught sight of a Blackfeet warrior reaching for his rifle. Instinct overruled diplomacy. He sprang up with a shout, waking the others.

A frantic struggle exploded in the half-light—men lunged for weapons, horses stampeded in panic, shouts echoed along the riverbank. Lewis found himself grappling with an attacker, knife flashing between them. Someone fired a musket in the chaos. Reuben Field chased down a fleeing warrior and wrested away his gun. In the confusion, two Blackfeet fell—one stabbed by Field in the chest, another shot by Lewis after raising a musket at him. It was fast, violent, and nothing like the careful negotiations of the night before.

Lewis's account in his journal is raw—a mixture of anger, fear, and deep regret. He wrote about gathering his men quickly, checking wounds, and realizing how close they'd come to being wiped out or losing all their horses. He described burning what the Blackfeet left behind to prevent pursuit. Most hauntingly, Lewis took one of Jefferson's peace medals—the very symbol of goodwill—and hung it around the neck of a dead Pikuni as proof that Americans had been there. Some say this was a warning; others call it a desperate message to future travelers or even an act of remorse.

The party fled at dawn with nerves frayed and spirits battered. Each mile away from that site felt like borrowed time. For days afterward, every shadow on the horizon looked like vengeance coming for them. The violence marked them all—Lewis especially seemed changed by it, weighed down by what he called "the melancholy event." This incident at Two Medicine River would become infamous as the only deadly conflict between Corps members and Native Americans during their entire trek. It shattered any illusion that diplomacy alone could guarantee safety or understanding.

The consequences rippled far beyond that summer morning. News spread among tribes on both sides of the mountains—a new kind of visitor had come, one who brought gifts but also guns and grief. The Blackfeet never forgot or forgave; relations between them and American explorers soured for decades after. Where once there had been a chance for trade or even fragile peace, suspicion now took root. This single night's violence would haunt not only Lewis but every American who crossed into Pikuni territory for years to come.

Yellowstone's Wonders – Clark's Route and New Discoveries

Clark's party moved away from the others with a sense of both curiosity and purpose, following the Yellowstone River into lands no one in the group had mapped before. The choice to strike out along this uncharted route was risky, but Clark believed that following the Yellowstone would fill in huge gaps on the map and open new possibilities for trade routes, settlement, and understanding of this wild region. The land itself seemed to change with every mile—one moment, you'd ride through open prairie thick with grass and wildflowers bending under the wind; the next, you'd find yourself peering down into deep canyons where the river twisted between walls of ancient stone.

Sometimes the water ran gently and wide, offering easy passage, but then it would narrow, churning white and loud, blocked by hidden rocks and sudden drops. The party often stopped just to stare at the strange shapes carved into the rock by wind and water. Those moments reminded everyone just how new and unpredictable this country remained.

One day, Clark's group came upon a striking sandstone butte rising above the plain. It looked almost like a giant's thumb pressed into the earth, a landmark impossible to miss from miles away. Clark felt moved to leave a mark here— something to say that they'd come this far. He used his knife to carve "Wm Clark July 25 1806" into the soft stone. Then he named the formation "Pompy's Tower" in honor of Sacagawea's little boy, Jean Baptiste, whom Clark called "Pompy" with affection.

This act wasn't just about pride or ego; it was a way of reaching through time, hoping that future travelers would see the inscription and know someone had passed this way and cared enough to tell them. The tradition of leaving your name on a landmark runs deep in human history—a blend of hope and loneliness, the urge to be remembered even when the rest of your story fades. The Yellowstone route revealed marvels no one from the Corps had witnessed before.

Clark carefully described the unusual rock formations—pillars shaped like towers, arches sculpted by centuries of rain, bluffs streaked with colors from minerals leaching through layers of stone. He made careful notes about their size, color, and location, aiming for accuracy so others could find them again. New plant life flourished along the riverbanks—willows thicker than a man's arm, wild roses bright against gray stone, strange berries that Sacagawea sometimes recognized and sometimes warned against. Wildlife was everywhere if you had sharp eyes. Pronghorn antelope bounded away at the slightest movement, barely more than tan blurs on the horizon. Wolves watched from a distance with pale yellow eyes, sometimes trailing the group in hopes of scraps. On some evenings, unfamiliar birds filled the air with calls so strange that even experienced hunters stopped to listen.

Not all discoveries brought joy or wonder. Horse thieves followed the group's trail for days, slipping in under the cover of darkness to cut out animals from the herd. One morning, Clark woke to find several horses gone—a loss that meant heavy packs had to be redistributed, and some men walked for miles on sore feet.

The landscape itself presented hazards at every turn. Rapids could flip a canoe without warning, sending men and supplies tumbling into freezing water. In narrow canyons, echoes sometimes made it hard to tell where danger lay.

Once, a sudden summer storm swept down from the mountains, turning dry creek beds into torrents and pinning the party on a patch of high ground for hours.

But what set Clark's crew apart was their stubborn resourcefulness. When horses vanished, they built crude sleds from tree limbs and hide to drag their gear across rough ground. When rapids threatened to smash boats against rocks, they worked together—sometimes waist-deep in swift water—to guide each craft through one at a time, using ropes and pure muscle. Even setbacks turned into lessons: Sacagawea showed how certain roots found along muddy banks could stave off hunger; York scouted for game in broken country where others feared to go. Every member pitched in—no task too small or undignified if it meant another safe mile eastward.

The landscape along Clark's route forced everyone to adapt quickly, think ahead, and rely on each other more than ever before. The sense of newness never faded: every sunrise brought sights no one expected and challenges that demanded courage and creativity. Even as exhaustion crept in, each person felt that something important was happening—not just for themselves but for anyone who would follow their tracks in years to come.

Grizzly Country – Survival and Peril on the Return

Late summer brought heightened peril to Lewis and Clark's parties as grizzly bears prowled the plains and river valleys, bolder and more numerous than ever. Both parties sensed the tension of sharing the wilderness with such fearless predators.

Ripening seeds and tall grass attracted game, which in turn drew in the bears. The Corps never relaxed its vigilance; this season, though, the danger grew sharper. At dawn, men read the land for fresh tracks—broad as a man's foot, claws dragging deep—while grizzly scat, riddled with berries and sometimes bison remnants, marked their paths. Nightly, sentries were doubled, camps pitched away from dense foliage and berry bushes.

Eastbound, bear encounters intensified. One afternoon, Lewis's group surprised a grizzly at a riverbank carcass. It charged immediately. Lewis fired, merely wounding it, but the bear thundered on, blood soaking its fur.

The group scattered, panic-stricken. Lewis ducked behind driftwood as others scrambled to reload. Only after several more shots did the bear finally collapse. Shaken, Lewis chronicled the ordeal that night, the fear still raw. The party lay awake as rain battered the tent, conscious of their narrow escape. Clark's group faced bears lured by the scent of meat or fish. York once spotted a grizzly's orange-lit eyes just outside the fire's glow.

On another night, chaos erupted when a bear tore into camp, Gass swearing he heard it snorting near his tent before it crashed through, scattering supplies and leaving twisted, clawed timber. Bears sometimes destroyed food stores before they could be saved; the men adapted by raising supplies into trees or suspending them on poles, hoping to defeat the grizzlies' uncanny sense of smell.

Their journals from this stretch pulse with adrenaline and dread, the writing terse and urgent. "The monstrous animal advanced upon us with astonishing rapidity," Lewis wrote. Clark's accounts confessed to fumbling with powder and relief that only arrived once a grizzly lay dead. These weren't just reports—they served as warnings, relaying the land's dangers with stark honesty.

As fear seeped into camp life, sleep grew rare, and tempers frayed. Every crack of a twig or distant growl sent the whole group to high alert. Rotating watch became a grim duty, exhaustion dragging on everyone. Yet adversity forged unity. Around the campfire, near-misses turned into tales, and even panic was recast in laughter—everyone had felt the fear. Surviving in grizzly country forced constant adaptation. Camps were erected on high ground, brush cleared in broad circles. Food was hidden in pits or hung high with improvised knots.

After a bear attack killed a packhorse, Clark tethered all animals close to sentries, with rifles always within reach. Rifle practice became a ritual, and extra care was taken to scrub pots and control cooking odors. Fires were built downwind and doused immediately after use. Tales from these months read like survival manuals: Drouillard once distracted a bear by tossing fish-oil-soaked moccasins from camp, giving others time to ready rifles and avoid a fight.

Reuben Field claimed he could detect bears by their "musk so strong it thickens the air," and his sense of approaching bears more than once spared the group an unpleasant surprise.

Everyone became skilled at reading signs—scat at water holes meant heightened alert at dusk, claw marks meant relocation before dark. Every day in grizzly country was earned by vigilance, quick adaptation, and teamwork refined by necessity. The gap between disaster and survival was precarious, shifting as fast as sunrise to sunset—a lesson none of them would ever forget.

The Long-Awaited Reunion – The Corps Regroups

Before anyone glimpsed a familiar paddle or heard a shouted call across the Missouri, every Corps member felt the anticipation of reunion. The agreed meeting point—where the Yellowstone meets the Missouri—was almost a leap of faith, given the lack of precise timing and unreliable maps. The river complicated plans: currents changed after rains, sandbars shifted, storms stranded one party for days as the other waited, anxious and hungry.

To bridge these distances, Lewis and Clark's teams left clever signs: burnt wood arranged in patterns, carved notches in trees, and messages under rocks. Scouts rode out at dawn, halting at every bend to search for smoke or a shining blade. Sometimes it seemed luck alone would reunite them.

When the parties finally spotted one another on opposite banks, shouts of relief cracked the air. Men who had faced death rushed to join boats, arms extended, laughter echoing. Questions and answers fired back and forth amidst tears and embraces: "Did you make it?" "Who's missing?" York nearly knocked Drouillard into the river with a joyful slap. Sacagawea gleamed as she held Pomp up for Clark. Even the stoic broke into grins or wiped away tears. The fear and hunger of separation vanished as everyone clamored to share their stories.

Lewis absorbed Clark's tale of the sandstone pillar he'd carved his name into; Clark's group listened wide-eyed to Lewis's account of conflict with the Blackfeet—the expedition's only bloodshed. Sorrow and joy mingled as each explained their separate routes, tales unspooling between laughter and silence.

Maps stretched out on driftwood; journals, soft from use, emerged from oilskin wraps for comparison by firelight. They pored over sketches, plant notes, and animal lists. Lewis showed pressed plants and recounted the northern prairies; Clark offered sketches of unusual rock, shared stories of stolen horses, and sightings of huge buffalo herds moving like clouds. Valuable native intelligence shifted hands: warnings about changing tribal moods, hunting tips, rumors of white traders from Spanish lands. Each report was judged for its role in survival—and for President Jefferson's needs back east. The camp buzzed with talk; even at night, men whispered over dying embers, piecing together all they'd seen and endured.

As supplies were counted, the mood sobered. Some faces were sadly absent—lost to accident or illness—but most were present, battered but alive. Powder horns were lighter, and clothing was little more than patched rags. Yet among their scattered gear, treasures remained: dozens of pressed plants, animal bones, labeled minerals, and journals filled with careful notes on weather, native customs, and celestial measurements. These provided a scientific legacy—one that the men joked would soon fill "Jefferson's bookshelf," but which gave their survival added meaning.

With the reunion, even reflection felt easier. Lewis wrote honestly about relief and exhaustion; the sight of friends had revived him after weeks of anxiety. Clark noticed his men were "cheerful," but noted in his journal he now felt older, aware of how thin the line between life and death truly was. Gass summed it up: "No man knows what he can bear until he has been tried." Around the fire, stories were retold not just for entertainment but to reconnect the group, stitching together their split experiences.

Each night, gratitude grew for simple amenities: hot food, dry ground, and friends close at hand. Camaraderie deepened; men who once bickered now shared rations without complaint and guarded each other's rest with new care. For every tale of hardship, someone pointed out a lucky break—a stray shot that saved a comrade, a break in a storm, even the humor found in mistakes.

This sense of shared fate became central: more than a comfort, it was a new understanding that the true accomplishment was not just reaching home, but returning as one, stories intact. On that riverbank, the Corps was no longer simply explorers but survivors, their map now marked not just by rivers and mountains, but also by shared hardships and discoveries.

Homeward Bound – Final Challenges and Reflections

Down the Missouri, water ran thick with memory, hope, and exhaustion. The Corps slipped past old campsites, each familiar bend in the river tugging at thoughts of home. Muscles ached from weeks of toil—shoulders burned, hands raw, boots long patched or replaced by scraps. Even as the river pulled them east, the days felt endless and heavy. Men spoke less of maps and more of beds, gardens, and families they'd left behind. Still, discipline held. Boats needed patching after long months battered by rocks and sun. Oars were repaired with driftwood and sinew. Provisions—dwindling but never quite gone—were shared out with care. Meat was smoked over small fires; corn was counted, then recounted, until every kernel felt precious. They bartered and traded among themselves, sometimes swapping tobacco for an extra slice of dried venison.

As they pressed on, new encounters with Native groups brought moments of both warmth and bittersweet parting. The Corps stopped in villages they'd passed before— Mandan, Hidatsa, Arikara—and found old friends waiting. Chiefs greeted them with open arms and keen eyes, some curious about what lay beyond the mountains and ocean.

Lewis and Clark offered gifts—shell beads, ribbons, medals—tokens that now carried the salt scent of the Pacific. The news they brought back was met with awe and sometimes disbelief: tales of giant trees, roaring surf, and strange animals living where the land fell away into mist and tide. Farewells came with honest regret. Some elders pressed advice and warnings on the men: dangers ahead, shifting alliances, reminders that nothing in this land stayed the same for long.

With each mile closer to settlements, a strange shift rippled through the Corps. Routines loosened; bedtime stories replaced strict watch schedules. No longer fighting for every scrap of comfort, some men even joked or sang. Others grew quiet, staring at the river or sky as if searching for answers to questions that had grown alongside them all this way. The transformation was visible—faces once hard set now softened with anticipation and worry. For so long, their world had been reduced to survival—weathering storms, chasing food, dodging threats seen and unseen. Now, minds wandered to what came next: Would people back home understand who they'd become? Would their stories be believed? Would they find a place among those who never left?

Clark wrote in his journal about nervousness creeping in as St. Louis drew near. Lewis sometimes stood apart on the deck, lost in thought as the banks grew busier with fields and scattered cabins. York's eyes searched for familiar faces on the horizon; Sacagawea stroked her son's hair and pointed out sights she recognized from before the westward trek began.

Anxiety rode alongside hope—would they be celebrated or forgotten? Would promises made along the way hold up under scrutiny? More than one man wondered if a hero's welcome awaited or if they'd simply fade back into the crowd.

The river shifted again—wider now, lined with boats and smoke curling from distant chimneys. On a clear September morning, church bells faintly echoed above the splash of paddles. St. Louis came into view at last: a jumble of rooftops, docks crowded with traders, children waving from muddy banks. The sight stopped conversation cold; hats came off, hands shook, some men wiped tears they hadn't planned on showing. Cheers broke out as word spread—a ragged band of explorers had returned from the Pacific! Crowds surged to the water's edge, pressing in with questions and shouts.

Lewis and Clark sent immediate dispatches to President Jefferson—quick notes carried by riders eager to share news of survival and discovery. Doctors checked wounds that had gone ignored for months; cooks offered fresh bread and salted pork; laughter spilled over from reunions as wives wept and children clung to fathers thought lost forever. For a few days at least, celebration swept through the settlement like wildfire.

In those first hours back among their own people, shock mingled with relief. Some men caught themselves glancing over their shoulders as if expecting trouble from behind—a habit slow to fade after so many months in an unfamiliar land. Others simply soaked in the sounds: dogs barking, bells ringing, the hum of voices eager for stories no one else could tell quite like them.

As this chapter closes, think about what it means to survive not just wild places but wild times—and to carry those changes home inside you. Ahead lies the reckoning of what was gained, what was lost, and how the story of Lewis and Clark would ripple far beyond their own lives into the story of a nation still finding its way west.

Chapter 8: Legacy of the Corps – Aftermath, Memory, and the Making of the American West

Lewis and Clark at Home – Fames, Failures, and the Price of Exploration

Imagine returning from years away, only to feel like a stranger in your own land. When Lewis and Clark re-entered St. Louis, excitement swept the city: banners waved, bells rang, crowds gathered to catch a glimpse of the men who had crossed an unimaginable continent. The Corps marched proudly, each man marked by both hardship and hope. In Washington, their arrival sparked a national celebration. Newspapers praised them, politicians toasted their success, and President Jefferson welcomed them as heroes. Banquets, medals, and speeches filled every evening—a wave of national gratitude that seemed, for a brief moment, to turn struggle into lasting glory.

Beneath the happy surface, however, reality was much more complex. Lewis, newly famous, was named Governor of Upper Louisiana—a powerful but exhausting position. The job came loaded with endless bureaucracy and political rivals eager to see him fail. With little experience in administration, Lewis became bogged down by paperwork, land disputes, and conflicts among settlers and officials. His dramatic decisions on the trail were replaced by the slow tedium of government. Isolated and surrounded by suspicion, Lewis struggled to adapt and found old camaraderie replaced by loneliness.

Clark's path differed but brought its own burdens. As an Indian agent and later governor of the Missouri Territory, Clark was valued for his steady judgment. He negotiated treaties, mediated conflicts, and worked constantly to keep the peace where settlement teetered on the edge of violence. Clark was better suited to public life, building relationships and maintaining friendships from the expedition. His reputation for fairness allowed him to withstand political turmoil.

Yet greatness came at a steep price for Lewis. The journals he'd so carefully written became a burden: publication was bogged down by delays, infighting, and lack of funds. Lewis faded from public attention as his account remained unpublished, feeling forgotten despite his sacrifices.

Lewis's problems ran deeper than professional frustration. He spiraled into depression, haunted by real and imagined failures. Friends worried about his drinking and erratic behavior. Gossip spread about debts and missed deadlines. Most days, he was unreachable and brooding. The spark that led him west now guttered. His final months ended in isolation on the Natchez Trace, his mysterious death officially ruled a suicide but still debated today—historians wonder whether illness or betrayal played a role.

Clark faced his own share of disappointment and personal loss, but he found new purpose: mentoring young explorers, caring for Sacagawea's son Jean Baptiste Charbonneau, and serving as a respected elder in St. Louis. Clark's home was filled with relics of his time on the trail.

Over time, the reputations of both men changed. Early Americans saw Lewis as a tragic genius—gifted but undone by private demons—and Clark as the pragmatic leader who built order from chaos. Later generations have reinterpreted their stories: Lewis sometimes appears as a pioneering scientist, sometimes as a failed politician; Clark's diplomatic legacy with Native nations has come under greater scrutiny, even as his mapping and leadership are still praised.

Today, their names fill the landscape—on highways, schools, museums, coins, and stamps. Some memorials show them as flawless heroes, while others highlight the costs and flaws of conquest. Recent research continues to reveal the real people behind the legend—their doubts, mistakes, and the heavy personal toll exploration demanded. The story of Lewis and Clark remains dynamic, shifting as new generations reinterpret what courage, failure, and discovery truly mean.

Sacagawea, York, and Beyond – The Lives and Legends of Key Members

After the expedition, Sacagawea's story became tangled in myth and conflicting accounts. Some say she died young at Fort Manuel in 1812, her grave shrouded in uncertainty, while others believe she lived until 1884, becoming a respected elder on Wyoming's Wind River Reservation. Even her name varies by tradition—Sacagawea,

Tsakakawea, Sakakawea—claimed by different communities. She has become a symbol: a bridge, a survivor, a mother, and a guide. In the early 1900s, women's suffrage supporters marched with her likeness, inspired by her supposed independence and courage. Later, her face graced the U.S. dollar coin, her steady gaze beside her infant son. Yet, her true self remains elusive; her voice lost to history, her story interpreted by others. Some view her as the expedition's quiet heart; others argue over how much influence she really had. Despite numerous statues and schools bearing her name, each retells a different version of who she was.

York's life after reaching the Pacific was marked by disappointment. Though he had trudged every mile, hunted, traded, and risked his life like any other member, freedom was denied him at journey's end. Clark refused to release York from slavery for years, claiming York needed time to adjust to city life. York pleaded for freedom, growing bitter and sometimes rebelling, but for a long time, remained Clark's property. Only after a persistent struggle did Clark eventually free himself. York's fate after emancipation is uncertain—he may have started a freight business in Kentucky, or perhaps lived among Native people on the plains; the records are inconclusive. What is clear is that York's pursuit of dignity and respect didn't conclude with the expedition.

Other Corps members left their own ambiguous marks. Toussaint Charbonneau continued his life as a guide, interpreter, and trader for decades, with a reputation that was both resourceful and unruly. Sacagawea's son, Jean Baptiste "Pomp" Charbonneau, received education and care from Clark in St. Louis, per Clark's promise to Sacagawea.

As an adult, Jean Baptiste lived a remarkable life—traveling Europe with a German prince, speaking several languages, and later returning to America as a mountain man, scout, and gold prospector before dying in the West he once crossed as an infant.

Patrick Gass survived into his nineties and published the first detailed account of the expedition, offering readers a glimpse into the expedition's reality beyond the settled frontier.

How Sacagawea, York, and others are remembered has shifted over time. Statues of Sacagawea are found from Oregon to North Dakota—sometimes depicted alone, with Lewis and Clark, or carrying her child. She is celebrated and critiqued: some see her as an emblem of female achievement, while others argue her story glosses over injustices faced by Native women. Statues of York have only recently become more visible, such as the one in Louisville, Kentucky, finally honoring his long-ignored contributions. His story now fuels movements for greater recognition of Black pioneers.

Today, schools, streets, and coins carry Sacagawea's and York's names. Their stories appear in murals, textbooks, and public memory—yet their legacies remain alive, evolving alongside our questions about memory, justice, and America's ongoing narrative.

Native Nations Remembered – Lasting Impacts and Changing Realities

The Lewis and Clark expedition is often remembered as a journey through uncharted wilderness, but its real legacy for Native nations is complex and ongoing. Initial meetings between the Corps and tribes were ceremonial and hopeful, with Lewis and Clark offering medals, flags, and promises. Native leaders responded with a mix of curiosity, caution, and opportunity. Gifts like beads, knives, and cloth brought immediate change, but deeper impacts—some visible and others gradual—soon followed.

Trade changed overnight. River villages saw an influx of steel tools, guns, kettles, and bright cloth. These weren't simply new possessions; they could shift regional power and disrupt traditional ways. But along with new goods came deadly diseases like smallpox and measles. The Mandan, once a central hub along the Missouri River, faced outbreaks that devastated families and forced survivors to abandon ancestral villages. Their story became a somber lesson echoed across the plains as diseases swept through established networks.

For the Nez Perce in the Northwest, early encounters with the Corps seemed positive. They provided food, directions, and shelter to the exhausted expedition. However, this trust gradually eroded as treaties were broken and violence erupted with the arrival of settlers. The Nez Perce War of 1877, which forced families from their lands, still resonates—Chief Joseph's famous words, "I will fight no more forever," capture the heartbreak of loss. The Shoshone, once thriving horsemen in the valleys, experienced similar displacement as hunting grounds were taken and gold-seekers flooded the region.

Some tribes faced exclusion from the outset. The Blackfeet, wary of the Corps, clashed violently with them and barred traders from their territory for years. Isolated from new trade yet surrounded by change, they resisted encroachment from trappers, soldiers, and settlers. On the lower Columbia, the Chinook quickly adapted to new trade but suffered heavily from epidemics and policies that eroded their sovereignty.

Major economic shifts rippled outward. Bison herds, once plentiful, dwindled as new rifles enabled mass overhunting. Traditional trade networks broke down or became fiercely competitive as outside traders imposed new terms. Some Native farmers benefited from novel crops and tools, but others lost fertile land due to forced treaties that drastically reduced their territory.

U.S. government policy soon followed exploration. Treaties were often disregarded, especially when gold was found or when settlers increased. The Mandan lost their homeland amid broken promises and expanding agriculture. Similar stories repeated across the West—displacement became common, and Native children were sent to boarding schools intended to erase Indigenous cultures. Blackfeet lands shrank steadily under pressure from ranchers and railroads.

Despite these challenges, Native nations did not disappear from history. Oral traditions preserved memories even when written accounts neglected Indigenous voices. Stories passed down through generations vividly recounted Lewis and Clark's visit—sometimes as friendship or cautionary tales, sometimes as lessons in survival or betrayal. These versions often sharply contrast with traditional textbooks.

In recent years, tribal historians and activists have worked to reclaim these stories. During the expedition's bicentennial (2004–2006), many tribes held their own events to honor ancestors and reflect on resilience and loss. The Nez Perce gathered by the rivers once traversed by the Corps, the Mandan, Hidatsa, and Arikara commemorated changes to their lands, and Chinook leaders advocated for renewed recognition. Today, you can visit tribal museums along the Lewis and Clark Trail or view online oral history projects where Native elders share their experiences firsthand. These efforts cannot erase past harms, but they offer opportunities for healing and a fuller understanding of what the expedition meant—and cost—for Native peoples.

Mapping the American West – Cartography and Scientific Legacies

Picture yourself holding a map of North America from the early 1800s. The western half is mostly empty, filled with wild guesses—mountains in the wrong places, rivers that don't exist, and a mysterious "River of the West" stretching all the way to the Pacific.

The Lewis and Clark expedition changed that, not just by walking across the land, but by recording what they saw with a level of detail and honesty that few could match. Their journals didn't just tell stories. They became blueprints for the West. Each observation, each sketch, every measurement—these raw details combined to shape how scientists, settlers, and leaders thought about this continent.

Lewis and Clark weren't content to scribble quick notes. They invented new ways to record what they found, packing along thermometers, sextants, specimen jars, and plant presses. If you've ever tried to take notes in the rain or describe a plant you've never seen before, you know how hard it can be. Now imagine doing it after days of hunger, with mosquitoes swarming and no guarantee you'll live to see your notes published. Despite those odds, they wrote down temperatures at sunrise, tracked river widths, pressed flowers between pages, and sent live animals—like prairie dogs—back east for Jefferson's curiosity cabinet. They asked questions about the people they met, too: What did the Mandan plant? How did the Nez Perce fish? How did horses change daily life for the Shoshone? This blend of natural history and ethnography was groundbreaking— turning their trek into a living laboratory.

Their approach to specimen collection set a standard for field science. Lewis's plant samples included dozens of species new to science; some became state flowers years later. Clark's sketches of animals like the pronghorn or bighorn sheep brought unknown creatures into American homes. Their mineral samples helped geologists understand mountain formation and river erosion in a time before much was known about these forces.

The journals' sheer volume—thousands of pages—meant that later botanists, zoologists, and geographers could revisit their work with fresh eyes. Even mistakes held value: when Lewis described the so-called "salt mountains" or tried to predict volcanic eruptions, he revealed how little anyone really knew—and how much more there was to learn.

Maps before Lewis and Clark were riddled with fantasy. Rivers sometimes flowed uphill on paper; whole mountain ranges appeared where only prairie existed. After their expedition, American cartography took a quantum leap forward. Clark's maps stitched together what had only been rumors—pinning down the course of the Missouri, revealing there was no single waterway connecting the Atlantic to the Pacific (the much-hoped-for Northwest Passage just didn't exist). Their painstaking work made it possible for traders, soldiers, and settlers to follow real routes instead of chasing legends. In fact, Clark's finished map was so influential that explorers used it for decades.

The expedition's scientific data didn't gather dust on shelves. Over time, universities and museums began collecting specimens, artifacts, and journals. Today, you can leaf through digitized versions of their original notes online—complete with corrections, margin doodles, and water stains from their travels. Annotated editions explain odd spelling or technical terms so you can follow along without a Ph.D. in botany or astronomy. Museums build interactive exhibits where you can see their tools or compare your own hand to Clark's measured footprints.

Scholars keep finding new insights by re-examining this massive archive. Sometimes, it's as simple as using modern DNA analysis to confirm the species Lewis described. Other times it's about understanding how the climate has changed by comparing today's plant ranges with those logged in 1805. The journals also serve as time capsules of language and culture—phrases in French, English, Nez Perce, or Shoshone pop up next to scientific notes.

If you're curious about how we know what we know about America's wild places—or why some rivers have their names—you can thank the careful work left behind by Lewis and Clark. It wasn't glamorous most days; it was mud, ink stains, frostbitten fingers, and sometimes heartbreak when specimens were lost or ruined. But the legacy they left is more than stories of adventure or survival—it's a foundation for science and discovery that still shapes how we see the West.

Trail of Memory – Monuments, Museums, and Modern Pilgrimages

If you've ever driven across the Midwest or Pacific Northwest, you might have spotted a brown sign with a feathered hatchet and the words "Lewis and Clark National Historic Trail." These markers follow the twisting course of rivers, wind through prairies, and snake over mountain passes, guiding travelers along the same path that the Corps of Discovery once carved into the land. The trail itself stretches more than four thousand miles, dotted with interpretive panels and weathered posts. For some, following these signs is a rite of passage or a family adventure—an act of curiosity and remembrance. For others, it's something deeper, a way to touch history by standing in the very places where decisions changed lives.

Major monuments now stand in cities and small towns from St. Louis to the Pacific Coast. In Portland, you'll find a bronze statue of Sacagawea gazing westward, her son bundled on her back. St. Charles, Missouri, boasts a dramatic tableau of Lewis, Clark, York, and even Seaman the dog, each figure frozen in motion as if still on the move. The Gateway Arch in St. Louis, while most famous as a symbol of westward expansion, also connects to this story—reminding visitors that the expedition began here and set the stage for everything that followed. Along riverbanks, atop bluffs, in public squares and schoolyards, these statues invite reflection on who gets remembered and how.

Museums and interpretive centers play a huge role in shaping public memory. At the Lewis & Clark Interpretive Center in Great Falls, Montana, you can trace your finger along a massive relief map or stare up at recreations of portage sleds and dugout canoes. Kids press their noses to glass displays full of animal pelts and hand-forged tools. Audio guides let you hear snippets from actual journals or tribal oral histories. Smithsonian exhibits feature rare artifacts—beaded belts, peace medals, battered notebooks—each item linking past to present.

National Park Service sites along the trail often include living history programs where costumed guides answer questions or demonstrate how to start a fire with flint and steel. These spaces are not just collections of objects; they are crossroads where facts meet imagination, where each visitor brings their own story.

The growth of heritage tourism has turned Lewis and Clark's route into a living ribbon of discovery. You'll see RVs parked near river landings in Nebraska, hikers tracing old portage trails in Montana, or school buses unloading chattering students at reconstructed forts. For many, retracing steps—whether by boat, bike, or foot—becomes an annual pilgrimage. Some people travel with meticulously highlighted guidebooks, others prefer to wander with only a map and a sense of wonder. Reenactment groups have paddled canoes in full costume, camping out under canvas, and eating dried bison meat just to get closer to that feeling of uncertainty and possibility. During the bicentennial celebrations from 2004 to 2006, parades filled small towns, while scholars and tribal leaders gathered for debates, music, storytelling, and remembrance.

The landscape of memory is alive, always shifting as new generations seek meaning in old stones and bronze faces. Even the most familiar statue can take on new significance when you stand before it on a rainy morning and imagine the river running high behind you, carrying voices from past centuries into your own day.

Lessons from the Journey – Leadership, Diversity, and the Spirit of Discovery

If you picture the Corps of Discovery together on a muddy riverbank, soaked and shivering but still focused on their common goal, you begin to see what made their success possible. Teamwork wasn't just a buzzword for them—it was survival. Each person brought something vital to the table, from Clark's calm navigation in a storm to Drouillard's sharp eyes on the hunt.

When disaster struck—boats capsized, storms raged, tempers frayed—what mattered most was how they worked together and adapted. No one could go it alone. They had to share burdens, listen to different voices, and trust each other's skills. That kind of unity doesn't come from luck; it's built day by day, through mistakes and effort.

When faced with the unknown, they didn't just freeze— they asked questions, took notes, collected samples, drew maps, and tried to understand what was around them. Scientific inquiry wasn't separate from daily life; it was woven into every step they took. That attitude matters today. Whether you're solving a family problem, starting a project at work, or tackling homework you don't quite get, curiosity is your best tool for moving forward.

Diversity among the Corps became both a blessing and a challenge. The team included men from different nations, classes, and backgrounds—French-Canadian voyageurs, American soldiers, York, Sacagawea, John Shields from Virginia, and more. This diversity helped them survive: Sacagawea's knowledge of edible plants saved lives; York's strength and unique perspective built bridges with Native nations; French speakers helped with trade. But inclusion had real limits. Not everyone got an equal say or reward—York remained enslaved for years after the expedition ended, and Sacagawea's voice was only recorded by others. These contradictions remind us that diversity alone doesn't guarantee justice or equality. For modern teams—whether in school groups, offices, or community organizations—real inclusion means careful listening, fair recognition, and shared opportunity.

It's easy to think that exploration is only about traveling far or discovering something new outside yourself. But the real legacy of this expedition lies in how it pushed ordinary people to grow in ways they never expected. In closing, the story of the Corps teaches us that leadership thrives on humility, perseverance grows through hardship, and real discovery starts with open minds and open hearts.

Conclusion

You've made it to the end of this wild, winding river of a story. If you've been reading late at night or turning these pages at the kitchen table, I want you to know I wrote this for you—for the curious, the history lovers, the families, the students, the teachers, and everyone in between who wants to feel the pulse of adventure that echoes across our country's past.

Let's take one last look at why the Lewis and Clark Expedition endures, why it still matters, and what it might mean for you and those around you. This journey was never just about two men heading west. It was about the birth of an American identity—imperfect, hopeful, and bold—and about the power of ordinary people facing the unknown together. Their travels shaped how Americans saw themselves: as explorers, learners, and sometimes, as neighbors or intruders in a land already full of life and history.

From the start, this expedition grew out of Thomas Jefferson's big, risky dream. He wanted to know what lay beyond the edge of the map. He wanted to build a nation that stretched from sea to shining sea. But his vision needed people willing to risk everything. Lewis, Clark, and their motley crew—soldiers, hunters, translators, an enslaved man, a teenage mother, and a baby—became the faces and hands of that vision. They were far from perfect, but they were stubborn, inventive, and open to learning.

We followed them as they packed their boats with supplies and hopes, rowed against the current of the Missouri, and shivered through a Dakota winter among the Mandan and Hidatsa. We saw them depend on the wisdom of Native nations, and we watched Sacagawea—barely out of girlhood herself—become a guide, a peacemaker, and a beacon. We didn't skip over York, whose strength, skill, and humanity were vital, even as his freedom was denied. We read about the Corps' constant challenges: storms, grizzlies, starvation, and the fear of getting lost in a land without roads or rescue.

We cheered with them when they glimpsed the Pacific at last, soaked and battered, but unbroken. And we trudged back east by their side, through heartbreak and hardship, split by dangerous choices and reunited by love of home. We saw how the return changed them, and how their story changed the nation—sometimes for better, sometimes for worse.

Their perseverance won the day, but not alone. Teamwork—real teamwork, where every voice matters and every skill counts—is what made the impossible possible. The Corps survived because they leaned on each other and learned from those around them, even when it meant setting aside pride or old fears. Their story also shows how much can be gained—and sometimes lost—when cultures meet. Sometimes there was friendship and learning. Sometimes there was misunderstanding, pain, or even violence. Honest storytelling doesn't shy away from these truths.

Curiosity was their compass. Every time Lewis or Clark stopped to sketch a plant or ask about a new word, they showed us the value of looking closer, of not pretending to know everything. I hope you feel inspired to face your own unknowns with that same mix of wonder and humility.

Thank you for coming along on this journey. I hope these pages have left you with a sense of awe, a few new questions, and maybe a little more courage to face your own wild unknowns. The story of Lewis and Clark belongs to all of us now—past, present, and future.

Thank you for completing this book.

I hope its contents meant a lot to you. As I mentioned earlier, when you can, please spend just a little time writing a review of *Across an Untamed Land: The Lewis and Clark Expedition.*

Many potential readers look at the quality and quantity of reviews that a book has earned, and the better reviews a book gets, the more Amazon prioritizes it on its website.

All you have to do is locate this book on Amazon and scroll down on the left to where it says "Write a customer review" and follow the directions to write a much-appreciated review. It doesn't have to be long. They recommend at least a few sentences.

Thanks much in advance, and for being part of this journey through America's history.

Blake Whitworth

A Blake Whitworth Chronicle of American Courage and Character

Each volume in this ongoing series explores a turning point in the making of the United States. Blake Whitworth is the author *of Lexington and Concord: The First Shots of Freedom, Across an Untamed Land: The Lewis and Clark Expedition, The Forgotten War of 1812, Newport's Gilded Age,* and *How the Pony Express Forged America's Frontier*. Known for vivid storytelling and meticulous research, he brings the defining moments of America's past to life with clarity and heart.

References

- *How the Louisiana Purchase Changed American History* https://www.monticello.org/thomas-jefferson/louisiana-lewis-clark/the-louisiana-purchase/
- *Expedition Members - Discover Lewis & Clark* https://lewis-clark.org/primary/members/
- *Meriwether Lewis's Packing List for the Expedition | Monticello* https://www.monticello.org/thomas-jefferson/louisiana-lewis-clark/preparing-for-the-expedition/lewis-s-packing-list/
- *American Indians and the Lewis and Clark Expedition* https://www.nps.gov/lecl/learn/historyculture/american-indians-and-the-lewis-and-clark-expedition.htm
- *The Lewis and Clark Expedition - Missouri ...* https://www.nps.gov/mnrr/learn/historyculture/the-lewis-and-clark-expedition.htm
- *York - Lewis & Clark National Historic Trail (U.S. ...* https://www.nps.gov/lecl/york.htm
- *The Otoes and Missourias - Discover Lewis & Clark* https://lewis-clark.org/native-nations/siouan-peoples/otoes-and-missourias/
- *May 14, 1804 | Journals of the Lewis and Clark Expedition* https://lewisandclarkjournals.unl.edu/item/lc.jrn.1804-05-14-1

- *Winter at Fort Mandan - Discover Lewis & Clark* https://lewis-clark.org/the-trail/fort-mandan/
- *Lewis and Clark - Knife River Indian Villages ...* https://www.nps.gov/knri/learn/historyculture/lewis-and-clark.htm
- *Sacagawea - Lewis & Clark National Historic Trail (U.S. ...* https://www.nps.gov/lecl/learn/historyculture/sacagawea.htm
- *Lewis & Clark among the Indians 5. ...* https://lewisandclarkjournals.unl.edu/item/lc.sup.ronda.01.05
- *Lewis and Clark depart Fort Mandan | April 7, 1805* https://www.history.com/this-day-in-history/april-7/lewis-and-clark-depart-fort-mandan
- *Great Falls Portage* https://www.nps.gov/places/great-falls-portage-mt.htm
- *Grizzly Bear Encounters - Discover Lewis & Clark* https://lewis-clark.org/sciences/mammals/bears/grizzly-bear-encounters/
- *Deciphering the Celestial Data - Discover Lewis & Clark* https://lewis-clark.org/sciences/geography/celestial-data/
- *Lewis & Clark among the Indians 6. Across the Divide* https://lewisandclarkjournals.unl.edu/item/lc.sup.ronda.01.06

- *Meeting with Cameahwait (U.S. National Park Service)* https://www.nps.gov/places/meeting-with-cameahwait.htm
- *Lewis and Clark (Lolo Trail)* https://www.nps.gov/parkhistory/online_books/lewisandclark/site4.htm
- *Lewis and Clark and the Nez Perce* https://www.nps.gov/nepe/learn/historyculture/lewis-and-clark.htm
- *Lewis and Clark prematurely celebrate their arrival at the ...* https://www.historylink.org/File/5360
- *Lewis and Clark Expedition, Part 9: Wintering at Fort Clatsop* https://www.americanacorner.com/blog/lewis-and-clark-fort-clatsop
- *History & Culture: People: Tribes - Lewis and Clark ...* https://www.nps.gov/lewi/learn/historyculture/histcult-people-tribes.htm
- *List of species described by the Lewis and Clark Expedition* https://en.wikipedia.org/wiki/List_of_species_described_by_the_Lewis_and_Clark_Expedition
- *The Return* https://www.nps.gov/articles/the-return.htm
- *Conflict with the Piegans* https://www.oregonhistoryproject.org/articles/historical-records/conflict-with-the-piegans/

- *Lewis and Clark (Pompeys Pillar National Monument)*
  https://www.nps.gov/parkhistory/online_books/lewi
  sandclark/site24.htm
- *August 12, 1806 - Discover Lewis & Clark*
  https://lewis-clark.org/day-by-day/12-aug-1806/
- *Lewis and Clark Expedition | Summary, History ... -
  Britannica*
  https://www.britannica.com/event/Lewis-and-
  Clark-
  Expedition#:~:text=Nevertheless%2C%20the%20e
  xpedition%20contributed%20significant,best%20av
  ailable%20until%20the%201840s.
- *Clark, Pomp, York, and Sacagawea*
  https://www.oregonhistoryproject.org/articles/clark
  -pomp-york-and-sacagawea/
- *The Expedition's Impact on Indigenous Americans*
  https://www.nps.gov/articles/the-expeditions-
  impact.htm
- *Scientific Encounters (U.S. National Park Service)*
  https://www.nps.gov/articles/scientific-
  encounters.htm

www.ingramcontent.com/pod-product-compliance
Lightning Source LLC
Chambersburg PA
CBHW071324140726
47996CB00005B/1804